A FAN'S GUIDE TO
BASEBALL
ANALYTICS

A FAN'S GUIDE TO
BASEBALL ANALYTICS

Why WAR, WHIP, wOBA, and Other Advanced Sabermetrics Are Essential to Understanding Modern Baseball

ANTHONY CASTROVINCE

SPORTS PUBLISHING

Sports Publishing books may be purchased in bulk at special discounts for sales promotion, corporate gifts, fund-raising, or educational purposes. Special editions can also be created to specifications. For details, contact the Special Sales Department, Sports Publishing, 307 West 36th Street, 11th Floor, New York, NY 10018 or sportspubbooks@skyhorsepublishing.com.

Sports Publishing® is a registered trademark of Skyhorse Publishing, Inc.®, a Delaware corporation.

Visit our website at www.sportspubbooks.com.

10 9

Library of Congress Cataloging-in-Publication Data is available on file.

Chart on page 154 courtesy of FanGraphs

The following tables, which appear in both the running text and appendix, are courtesy of FanGraphs: OBP, OPS, ISO, wOBA, BsR, wRC+, OPS+, ERA+, WHIP, GSc, FIP, FB%/LD%/GB%/IFFB%, K%/BB%, K/BB HR/FB, LOB%, IRS%, DRS/UZR, Inside Edge, DER, and WPA

Cover design by 5mediadesign

Print ISBN: 978-1-68358-344-8
Ebook ISBN: 978-1-68358-345-5

Printed in the United States of America

For my girls—Kate, Ella, and Lily—who give me incalculable joy.

And for my Dad, who is fond of saying "Statistics are for losers," but has promised to read this book anyway.

Table of Contents

Introduction
Stats What I'm Talking About—Why Baseball's "Nerdy" Numbers Are Worth Learning

"The nerds are ruining baseball!"

Right away, I knew this emailed response to an article I had written for MLB.com on the 2018 National League Most Valuable Player race was not going to be filled with the usual flattery about my flowing prose and rugged good looks.[1]

"An article based solely on 'advanced metrics' is nauseating," the writer of this maddened missive continued. "Most people don't know what any of those numbers mean, including me, and I've been a CPA and financial analyst."

Two thoughts crossed my mind when I received this email:

1. Does the use of the past tense of "I've been" mean this gentleman is retired from CPA and financial analyst work, or did he become so disenchanted with advanced mathematical concepts that he decided to leave the profession ahead of schedule?
2. When did I become a nerd? How did this happen?

We are all capable of myopic and mistaken perceptions of self, of not comprehending how our words, actions, or presence is observed by others. And right then, reading that email from that

---

1   In truth, I eagerly await the first such email.

retired-or-embittered former CPA and financial analyst, it hit me: despite a general childhood aversion to math and an earnest intent on becoming a storyteller and not a statistician, I had, indeed, inadvertently wandered into and purchased property in the Valley of Nerdom!

This was not the path I set for myself in high school, where quite literally my only lasting memory from Algebra II class was arriving early on an exam day, prior to any other students or the teacher, and set the alarm on the clock radio (a makeshift replacement for the broken clock on the wall) to go off about 20 minutes before the end of the period. My classmates and I were mid-quiz, preoccupied with polynomials, when, to my delight and surprise, the alarm that I thought I had set to "BUZZER" turned out to be tuned to "RADIO." Instead of a bothersome beep, something even better blared . . .

"LOVE SHACK!" wailed the buoyant voices of the B-52s. "BABY, LOVE SHACK!"

Ah, I had been blessed by the gods of algebraic intervention to have landed not just on our local pop station, Q104, and not just on the B-52s' irresistible signature single, but on that millisecond of muteness in the song between Cindy Wilson yelling, "Tin roof . . . rusted!" and the drum kicking in the final chorus. This amalgam of a broken clock, a rousing radio, and a new wave band breaking the silence with its silly song was as close to a perfect achievement as I could ever hope to attain in this warped world.

Seriously, though, that's all I retained from math class.

Sports writing was, in my ardent estimation, the only fulfilling option on the career menu—a means of satiating my curiosity about the human condition, appeasing my attraction to the script-proof and aesthetic drama of athletic events, and distributing that little dose of dopamine which comes with a fun turn of phrase within a Microsoft Word document. I wanted to retell results with such forcefulness, such sentiment, such captivating eloquence that even those who attended or otherwise witnessed the event in question would gain new perspective on the proceedings.

If that meant tossing in a few field-goal percentages or left-on-base counts, so be it.

It just so happens that MLB.com had an internship available for a cub reporter who saw dugout access, internet bandwidth, and a $7-an-hour paycheck as a *Godfather* offer. Thus began a long love affair with the unusual-but-unmistakable rhythms of the baseball beat. The late nights and crazy flights. The colorful characters. The indecipherable-to-outsiders lingo. When you cover a sport that consumes the calendar with a series of tomorrows—one that offers its inhabitants the chance to repeat past fortunes or repair past flaws, all while humbling even the most blessed of the bunch—it can teach you a lot about life itself.

But while this wasn't what you'd call a Chevy Chase–esque, "It was my understanding there would be no math" scenario (baseball, after all, is the most numbers-driven competition this side of a grade school Mathlathon), I never anticipated that the game would become so consumed by an avalanche of analytics, above and beyond the back-of-the-baseball-card stuff I was more readily familiar and comfortable with. In my time around the game, front offices have been taken over by the disrupters, the data scientists, the men and women who—were it not for that aforementioned allure of performance art unfolding on fresh-cut grass and dirt diamonds—would be splitting atoms or launching rockets. Not taking the time to understand the mathematical rationale behind their moves would have been journalistic malpractice on my part.

And while I was trying to make sense of this sport by counting on my fingers, some truly intelligent scribes—people who would probably bring as much value to a front office as they do to a front page—were writing articles that challenged my preconceived notions, opened my eyes to concepts I had never considered, and just generally ran laps around anything analytical I could attempt to offer an audience. It didn't mean I couldn't still wax poetic and post pieces that capture the soul—not the stats—of the sport. But I would be selling myself—and my readers—short if I didn't take the time to figure out what WAR, WHIP, wOBA, and the like mean and how they relate to player performance, instead of just making lame jokes about how silly they sound.[2]

So yeah, maybe I did become a bit of a nerd. Or more accurately, I learned to appreciate and even enjoy what the actual nerds—the folks whose true love of this great game compelled them to craft ways of contextualizing it—have to offer.[3]

Yet where I whiffed in that aforementioned MVP piece (and, I'm sure, many others) was in citing stats such as Christian Yelich's fWAR, Nolan Arenado's wRC+, or Paul Goldschmidt's OPS+ without properly, even if briefly, explaining what they mean to the readers who might not be familiar with them. Even stats like on-base percentage and slugging percentage, which have been around for decades and are considered rudimentary for some, are not fully grasped by others. Heck, Atlanta Braves manager Brian Snitker told me in 2019 that he still likes to write his players' batting averages (alongside various matchup data) on his lineup cards before games, just because of the familiarity factor.

"I'm learning the OPS's and stuff like that," said Snitker, who coached or managed in the Braves' system for thirty-five years before getting his first big-league managerial opportunity. "But I still see certain things and view it certain ways because I've done it for a long time."

---

2 They *do* sound silly, though. Let's be honest.

3 In that vein, I strongly recommend Keith Law's *Smart Baseball*—a book that, like this one, contains definitions of some advanced stats but operates less as a glossary and more as a thesis on why and how sabermetrics has improved the game of baseball and where the sport is headed.

I get it. One hundred percent.[4] And my sincere hope is that nothing in this book comes off as preachy, pompous, or condescending. Unfortunately, that is where some analytics-driven content veers off course; essentially telling generations of fans they are dumb just because they still like to converse about the game using averages or RBIs. It's a turn off and, given all the entertainment options available in the present day, everybody with a vested interest in baseball should focus on inclusivity, not exclusivity.

So I'm here to build you up, not break you down. While there *is* plenty of math in this book (sorry), I'm presenting it as casually as I can. Plus, when things get super-duper complicated, I'll give you a brief lay of the land instead of wandering too deep into the woods and weeds.

Fair warning, though, that doing so will involve a difficult discussion or two. For those who do view old stats as the gold standard, the first section of this book will require an open mind as I offer examples of why the aforementioned averages and RBIs—as well as wins, saves, and errors—can unfortunately skew your perception of a player and/or point you in the wrong direction.

Then we're going to get into the "advanced" numbers, divvied up into sections (offense, pitching and defense, team stats, and then some fun, context-driven data points) and, for those who read from beginning to end, gradually building up our tolerance to tricky digits along the way. We'll discuss what they mean, how they're calculated, and how they were created. I won't cover every single metric that's out there, because there are tons (we're talking about WAR and cleats, not *War and Peace*), but I'm going to cover all the stuff you are most likely to see referenced in media coverage of MLB.

Consider this book a conversational glossary. Not every chapter is for everybody. You can turn to whichever ones suit your

---

4 Hey, look, a stat!

needs at a given time, and you can use the handy charts at the back of the book as a reference point whenever you read or hear a certain stat cited in media coverage. If you've already grasped and mastered something contained herein, by all means flip to a stat that's new to you.[5]

If it's *all* new to you, well, hop in my Chrysler, it's as big as a whale, and it's about to set sail.[6] And if you happen to know that former CPA's address, let's swing by and pick him up, too.

---

5 Just know you might miss some sweet puns.
6 I will not apologize for getting "Love Shack" stuck in your head.

SECTION 1
Behind in the Count—The Trouble With the Old Stats

Scientists, psychologists, and researchers of many types and stripes have grappled with the difficulty of changing people's minds. We humans are generally intransient. We believe what we believe, and what we tend to believe is what we were raised to believe: the precepts and presumptions that were forged in our minds at early ages.

That locked-in logic can be difficult to shake, and I freely admit to not being qualified enough in the fields of behaviorism or hypnotism to influence others. I can't even get my young daughter to go to bed on time.

Still, in this opening section, I'm going to do my best to explain why some of the baseball math we have long turned to as our mental bread and butter is actually bad for our health. Well, OK, not *literally* bad for our health (to my knowledge, you can't overdose on RBIs), but, at the very least, hindering our understanding of what we're watching.

Stats such as batting average, RBIs, errors, wins, and saves are all baseball backbones, which is why I still tend to include them in my writing—only because I know my readership is comfortable and familiar with them. But not acknowledging their faults and trusting them as the be-all and end-all is a mistake. Allow me to explain why.

AVERAGE? MORE LIKE BELOW AVERAGE!

Why Batting Average Doesn't Tell Us Enough About Batter Performance

In health terminology, you are what you eat.

In baseball terminology, you are what you hit.

Or, at least, that's what we were groomed to believe when we first fell in love with the game. If you were a baseball player in the twentieth century, your batting average was so much a part of your identity it might as well have been printed not just on your baseball card, but your driver's license as well.

If batting average isn't the most famous statistic in all of professional sports, it's definitely in the conversation. Even non-baseball fans are familiar with the concept of hits divided by at-bats. The phrase "batting .500" has been used to describe many situations in which we succeed in one element of a task while failing at another.

> **Example:** You aced your history test but failed your chemistry test? Hey, you're batting .500!

Batting average has endured because of its easy application both to our own lives and to our evaluation of player performance.

We all know what a .400 hitter is. That's the gold standard. That's Ty Cobb and Ted Williams. That's the number that the likes of Tony Gwynn, George Brett, and Rod Carew chased in the homestretch of seasons of yore. Back in the late 1800s, Ward McAllister, the self-appointed arbiter of New York society, coined the phrase "The Four Hundred" in reference to those he deemed to be the only 400 people in the city who truly mattered. That same number—albeit with a different decimal place—has come to represent baseball's upper crust as well.

We're also all familiar with what it means to be a ".300 hitter." That means you excel at your craft. It means you have crossed some imaginary-but-important threshold that those who had the unmitigated gall to hit .299 or less can only dream about. You want to go to the Hall of Fame? You'd better hit .300.[1]

And we also know what a .200 hitter is. That's the dreaded "Mendoza Line." To tread that line is to be the definition of incompetence. To fall below it is to be in some sort of nether region in which your season—if not your very soul—is irredeemable.

These are the basic batting average breakdowns that have been handed down from generation to generation.

Alas, they are mostly baloney.

Batting average is so deeply ingrained into our baseball psyches, so strongly associated with our scoreboards, so natively intrinsic in how we define a ballplayer that to suggest it simply does not matter is, to some, an almost atheistic assertion.

But let's try anyway.

Batting average's simplicity is the backbone both of its ability to be embraced by the masses and its inability to tell us much about a particular hitter. There have been .400 hitters who weren't even the most productive players in their league in a given season, and there have been .300 hitters whose performance, at large, did not rate as positively as players whose averages had a "2" right after the decimal.[2]

---

1 Actually, only two Hall of Famers—Roberto Alomar and Enos Slaughter—did exactly that, while no Hall of Famer is in with a career average of exactly .299. Take that worthless trivia and do with it what you will.

2 In fact, since 1931, there have been 31 instances where a player batted under .300, yet won the MVP Award. And no, I will not list them all.

Heck, even the Mendoza Line is a lie, because Mario Mendoza, the namesake of that lamentable label, was himself a career .215 hitter, and never hit .200 for a single season. The "Uecker Line," for beloved Milwaukee Brewers broadcaster and career .200 hitter Bob Uecker, would arguably be a more appropriate appellation.[3]

The trouble with batting average is not what it tells you but what it does *not*. It's useful as a small piece of the puzzle, but there are far better metrics to assess offensive performance, which we will cover later in this book.

In the meantime, let's consider what are, for all intents and purposes, the ten ways a trip to the plate can end:

1. Hit
2. Walk
3. Plain-old out (strikeout, groundout, flyout, popout)
4. Sacrifice bunt
5. Sacrifice fly
6. Hit by pitch
7. Fielder's choice
8. Reach on error
9. Dropped third strike
10. Defensive interference[4]

Again, batting average is hits divided by at-bats. But five of the outcomes listed above—drawing a walk, hitting a sacrifice fly, executing a sacrifice bunt, getting hit by a pitch, and reaching on interference—are not counted as at-bats. You know that phrase "a walk is as good as a hit?" Apparently, the statistician Henry

---

3 "When I came up to bat with three men on and two outs in the ninth, I looked in the other team's dugout and they were already in street clothes."—Bob Uecker, *Baseball Digest*, June 1972

4 We can quibble over how to break those down and perhaps come out with a longer or shorter list, depending on your preference. But, as David Letterman can attest, lists of ten work best.

Chadwick, who is widely credited with "inventing" batting average and many other baseball stats, did not agree with that sentiment. But then again, the game Chadwick was watching—especially in those years when hitters could direct the pitcher where they wanted the ball thrown—was very different from the one we're watching today. So let's not hold it against him, OK?

Batting average covers only five of the ten potential outcomes on our list.[5] And while a .500 average would be pretty awesome as a player, it's not much of a showing for a stat so commonly cited as baseball gospel.

The so-called "batting title" goes to the hitter from each league who has the highest batting average, yet you need 502 *plate appearances* (or an average of 3.1 per team game in a 162-game season) to even qualify for the title. So the five outcomes described above that, for whatever reason, don't matter when tabulating batting average suddenly matter when assessing who has the best batting average.

It's enough to drive you batty.

That batting average turns a blind eye to so many outcomes is not even the greatest flaw in its role as a batter barometer. No, the greatest flaw is the implied insistence that all hits are created equal. A grand slam that soars out of the stadium and a weak dribbler off the handle of the bat that somehow results in a single (which is often followed with the jokey remark that it is "a line drive in the box score") are the exact same thing in terms of how they affect a player's batting average. That is askew.

And yet, for decades, this was the stat we used to judge a player's worth as a professional hitter. It's why player-turned-performance coach Steve Springer, who had a cup of coffee in the big leagues and worked as a coach and scout in the Toronto Blue Jays' system, once told me, "The batting average is Satan."

---

5 A fly out that scores a run does not negatively impact a hitter's batting average, but a groundout that scores a run does. Put that in the category of, "Things that make you go hmmm."

"It's the biggest trap in baseball," Springer continued. "You can do everything right and go 0-for-4. How can that be? You can hit three rockets right at somebody. The pitcher knows you beat him, the pitcher's mom knows you beat him, but your confidence goes down because your batting average goes down? How does that make sense?"

It doesn't. And thankfully, in recent years, we've been treated to new ways of accounting for these unrewarded "rockets." Though batting averages have been broadcast in every baseball stadium in the world for as long as anyone can remember, there's another number on the board that matters more: Runs. After all, they *do* decide the result. And unfortunately for batting average devotees, there are offensive statistics that do a far better job telling us how much a player contributes to the run-scoring process.

By the time you're done reading this book, you'll be more familiar with those better offensive evaluators—stats such as OBP, wOBA, and wRC+.

For now, just know that average is mediocre at best.

Steady As She Goes

When is a .247 batting average impressive? When you finish with that exact same figure *four seasons in a row*.

Slugger Khris Davis achieved this unusual feat from 2015 to 2018, becoming the first player in MLB history to have the same batting average in four straight seasons. The only other player to do it three straight years was Mookie Wilson, who hit .276 each year from 1983 to 1985.

While Davis's batting average was south of the major-league average in each of those four seasons, other numbers such as OPS, OPS+, and wRC+—all of which we'll cover later in this book—painted a rosier picture of a player who was, in fact, well above average in terms of run production.

RBI: REALLY BAD IDEA?

Why RBIs Don't Really Tell Us Much About a Hitter's Ability to Produce

Tension arose at a meeting of the Frontier Girls.

It was time for the annual cookie-selling competition, and the troop leader, Peggy, handed out the assignments for where the scouts would set up shop. She assigned a girl named Ally to a location outside of Petey's Mufflers, which was roundly known in scout-cookie-selling circles as a dead spot. As it turns out, the smell of exhaust and cinnamon swirl cookies doesn't mix particularly well, and Petey's didn't have much foot traffic.

Peggy, meanwhile, in a bold and blatant display of nepotism, had given her own daughter, Molly, the plum assignment of selling outside of Marco's Pizza, a popular restaurant. As dozens of patrons picked up a piping-hot pie with their stomachs rumbling, the cookies would practically sell themselves.

Ally's father, Ray, was upset. A major award (a beach chair . . . complete with an umbrella!) was on the line. The girls would be judged by the number of cookie boxes hocked, and Molly had a distinct advantage over the other contestants—especially Ally. It wouldn't necessarily matter if she didn't have much of a sales pitch. She would have more opportunities to cash in.

The above is a description of an episode of *Everybody Loves Raymond*, and it has absolutely nothing to do with baseball (well, aside from Ray Romano's character being a sportswriter). But it's a farcical situation that helps explain the fallacy of RBIs.

For a long time, in my writing, I revolted against the use of the plural "RBIs" because the correct plural is Runs Batted In, not Runs Batted Ins. It was a small bit of rebellion in an otherwise complaint life. But you can only fight The Man so much. My editors would routinely add the "s" after the fact, citing the *Associated Press Stylebook*. I've given up the fight, but I still hold out hope that the guiders of the *Stylebook*, who recently proved their attention to the important matters in life when they made "BLT" an acceptable first reference to a bacon, lettuce, and tomato sandwich, will address this serious issue.

RBIs, much like cinnamon swirl sales in the Frontier Girls competition, are a product of opportunity. For as long as we've been following baseball, we've used the RBI as a quantification of a player's ability to produce. And, to be sure, there have been many players who racked up RBIs so consistently in their careers that they give the illusion of having a knack for clutch knocks. Some of these players received an inordinate amount of money largely on their reputation as RBI assembly lines, cranking out runs as if they were widgets.

Funny thing, though, about RBIs: It's a lot easier to compile them when the guys hitting in front of you get on base. Just like Molly was set to benefit from the unrelated attraction of Marco's Pizza, players with high RBI totals benefit from the foot traffic provided by peers who can get themselves in scoring position. Though solo homers are good for a single RBI, it takes a team effort for a player to achieve a lofty RBI mark. So the

RBI can hardly be trusted as a useful stat in assessing individual accomplishment.[6]

And I don't know how you feel about this, but, to me, when people refer to RBIs as "ribbies," the stat goes from untrustworthy to flat-out cringeworthy.[7]

It was plenty cringeworthy in 2017, when people would point to Los Angeles Angels slugger Albert Pujols's RBI accumulation (he finished with 101) as some sort of evidence that, while his bat was obviously nowhere near the MVP caliber of old, he still brought a lot of value to the Angels lineup; that he could still come through "in the clutch."

"The guy is, what, fourth or fifth in our league in RBIs?" Angels manager Mike Scioscia told the *Los Angeles Times* midseason (Pujols finished 11th). "Those guys don't fall off of trees. This guy has done a good job for us."

To be clear, I have great respect for Albert Pujols. Drafted by the St. Louis Cardinals in the 13th round in 1999, he made himself into one of the greatest right-handed hitters the game had ever seen. A copy of this tome will be in a vintage bookstore by the time his 2005 NLCS homer off the Houston Astros' Brad Lidge lands. He's a legend, through and through.

But in 2017, at the age of 37, Pujols was a bit of a black hole at the plate. He got on base in less than 30 percent of his plate appearances. His power production, as measured by his slugging percentage, was only slightly better than the likes of Alcides

---

6 Though at least it's better than Game-Winning RBIs (GWRBI), which was adopted as an official stat in 1980, only to be abandoned by 1989. The GWRBI was credited to the player who notched the RBI that gave his club a lead it never relinquished. But the flaw was revealed in its very first usage, when the Cincinnati Reds' George Foster was credited with the GWRBI for a first-inning RBI double in what turned out to be a 9–0 Reds victory over the Atlanta Braves on Opening Day 1980. Not exactly clutch stuff.

7 I can acquiesce on RBIs, but not on "ribbies."

Escobar and Billy Hamilton—players whose values rested solely in their gloves or legs. Pujols grounded into 26 double plays, leading all of baseball. For a bat-only player who logged 143 games as a designated hitter and just six as a first baseman, Pujols's production was a net negative. The Angels would have been better off rotating other players in and out of the DH spot to give them rest from the rigors of the field. But with more than $100 million still remaining on their preposterous pact with Pujols, that was simply never going to happen.

Meanwhile, on Pujols's own team, there was Mike Trout. In five of Trout's first seven full seasons (including 2017, when he missed six weeks with an injury), he fell short of 100 RBIs. There was a time (and maybe, to some fans, we're still in that time) when the lack of triple-digit totals would have been used as evidence that Trout lacks some sort of clutch gene—the one that science and nature somehow implanted in Pujols.

Nah. The only thing Mike Trout lacked was . . . Mike Trout batting in front of him.

Pujols had that luxury, Trout didn't. It's really that simple.

Because Trout missed time with an injury in 2017, let's compare his 2018 to Pujols's 2017, as they logged a similar number of plate appearances (PAs) in those two years. Pujols had far more instances in which he came to the plate with runners on base (ROB) and runners in scoring position (RISP):

Player, Season	PAs	RBIs	PAs w/ROB	% of PAs w/ROB	PAs w/RISP	% of PAs w/RISP
Pujols, 2017	636	101	315	49.5	195	30.7
Trout, 2018	608	79	231	38.0	130	21.4

So, how did they fare in their respective RBI opportunities? Look, we've already addressed the flaws of batting average, but, in the interest of keeping this simple before we delve into more nuanced numbers, we can use that stat to make a pretty clear illustration of the heart of the matter here:

Player, Season	BA w/ROB	BA w/RISP
Pujols, 2017	.247	.264
Trout, 2018	.325	.346

Tell me: Which player was more "clutch?"

Pujols's high 2017 RBI total provided little insight into his season, and the same goes for Trout's 2018 total. In this book, we'll cover the many advanced metrics that do a much better job of evaluating their seasons. For now, it's clear: Pujols was selling cookies outside the pizza shop, while Trout was stuck at the muffler shop.

Triple Frown

The allure of the Triple Crown—that rare achievement of leading the league in batting average, home runs, and RBIs—lives on because we learned about it roughly the same time we were told of Santa Claus. And just as leaving milk and cookies for a stranger breaking into your home in the middle of the night makes little sense, so, too, does putting an enormous amount of emphasis on these three categories taken in tandem.

The problem with the Triple Crown is, appropriately, threefold:

1. As we discussed, batting average treats all hits as equals and ignores non-hit-related means of getting on base. So it's not a great measure of a player's overall skill set.

2. RBIs (also flawed) and home runs are much too intertwined to tell us much about the depth and dimension of a player and, therefore, to represent two-thirds of the Triple Crown. There have been 108 instances in the modern era (going back to 1901) in which a player has led his league in both home runs and RBIs. Obviously, a good number of seasons featured a player leading his league in those two categories in both leagues. But on average, you've had about a 45 percent chance in a given year of a player accomplishing that feat. Not exactly rare air.

3. Best we can tell, horse racing's Triple Crown (winning the Kentucky Derby, Preakness Stakes, and Belmont Stakes) was recognized first. The *New York Times*, for the record, began regularly referencing the racing Triple Crown in 1930—the year Gallant Fox achieved the feat. It didn't reference it in baseball until 1937—the year St. Louis Cardinals outfielder Joe Medwick pulled it off. The racing Triple Crown requires a horse to run three times in five weeks at three different tracks with three different distances—overcoming all variables related to weather, the racing field, jockey strategy, etc. With only one shot at each event, everything must play out perfectly. Is winning the baseball Triple Crown as difficult as winning the horseracing Triple Crown? I, for one, say "neigh!"

TO ERR IS HUMAN

But the Error's Deceptive Defensive Data—and Influence on ERA—Is Not Divine

It was the fifth inning . . . too early for a national audience to get in-game alerts on their smartphones that something special was happening, but late enough for those inside the Oakland-Alameda County Coliseum to know that something special was possible.

Sean Manaea was on the mound for the Oakland A's, facing a loaded—and eventually World Series–bound—Boston Red Sox team that had won eight straight and 17 of its first 19 games of the season, with the league's most runs scored and highest batting average, on-base percentage, and slugging percentage.

And he had yet to allow a hit.

The left-handed Manaea was not the guy you would have picked for the first serious no-hit bid of the 2018 season. He was good, but rather inconsistent. On this April night, however, his changeup and slider—the pitches Manaea employed to make up for his lack of a truly fiery fastball—were on point, and the Boston bats were befuddled.

Then, with two outs in the top of the fifth, Red Sox catcher Sandy León lifted a fly ball to shallow left field. Oakland shortstop Marcus Semien ranged toward it with his back to the infield. Later, the advanced Doppler data available from MLB's Statcast system would reveal that balls hit with this exit velocity (68.5 mph) at this angle (42 degrees) to this distance (211 feet) fall in for a hit 37 percent of the time—or good for a .370 batting average. Not too shabby. But Semien, an agile defender, was able to get a glove on the ball while on the run.

However, the ball fell to the ground.

Inside the press box, Art Santo Domingo—a longtime, part-time official scorer for the A's and San Francisco Giants—reviewed the video replay and deliberated for a moment. Finally, he leaned into the small microphone used to relay his ruling to the writers and broadcasters on the press level.

"Error," he said.

The no-hitter was intact, and would remain so through the ninth. Manaea had etched his name into the record books, but only with the help of the scorebook. In fact, in the press conference after the game—after his teammates had mobbed him at the mound and then covered him in Gatorade and whipped cream and crowned him with a Dubble Bubble bucket—Manaea himself admitted he didn't realize it was a no-hit bid until late in the game.

"I thought it was a hit," he said of Semien's error. "Until the eighth, I thought it just, like, was a one-hitter. I looked up in the eighth and saw there were still zeros and was like, 'whoa, weird.'"

The error—and how it is applied—is weird. And it shouldn't be taken seriously as a definition of defensive ability.

On the day before Manaea's no-no, the Padres' Tyson Ross had his own flirtation with history. Facing the D-backs in Arizona, he was four outs away from the first no-hitter in San Diego Padres franchise history when pinch-hitter Christian Walker sent a fly ball to center field. Franchy Cordero misread the play and took a bad route on the ball, which flew over his head and outstretched glove to fall in—not only breaking up the no-hitter but also the shutout, as Walker's double had driven home a baserunner aboard via a walk.

The Statcast data was especially stark on that play. The system (don't worry, we'll get into Statcast's offerings later) tracks how far an outfielder had to go, how much time he had to get there, which direction he had to travel, and his proximity to the wall to come up with a stat called Catch Probability, or the likelihood that a batted ball to the outfield will be caught.

That fly ball sent toward Cordero had a Catch Probability of . . . 99 percent!

So do you see the difference here? Similar situations (a no-hit bid), similar plays (a fielder ranging back with his back to the ball). Semien tried to flag down a ball that falls in for a hit 37 percent of the time and was punished with an error for getting his glove on it, while Cordero screwed up the route on a routine play but didn't get punished with the error simply because he didn't get a glove on it.

And history was affected both times.

That was just one 24-hour period early in the 2018 baseball season. Though the weight of a no-no obviously isn't always hanging in the air, this kind of stuff—a person in the press box contemplating that thin line between hit and error—happens every single day on the schedule. The error is a judgment call made by a human being far away from the actual action. Sometimes players even successfully appeal the judgment by having their lawyers— er, excuse me, their team public relations staff—speak up on their behalf.

Yet, for some reason, we have been trained to employ the error as an evaluation tool.

Time was, the error had a purpose in relaying the results of a ballgame. In the 1800s, when the ball was almost perpetually in play and fielders' gloves were small slices of leather barely bigger than their actual hands, there were errors aplenty. But as pitching, defense, athletic ability, and equipment evolved, the error counts slowly faded:

1870s: 10.5 per game
1880s: 8.2 per game
1890s: 5.7 per game

1900s: 3.8 per game
1910s: 3.3 per game
1920s: 2.6 per game
1930s: 2.3 per game
1940s: 2.1 per game
1950s: 1.8 per game

The average number of errors has been comfortably below 2.0 ever since. In fact, in the 2010s, there were just 1.2 errors per game, which means the typical team made one about every other day. And because so much error adjudication comes down to guesswork anyway, analysts like MLB Network's Brian Kenny have been outspoken against the sheer existence of the error. They argue that every ball put in play that falls in should—especially in this high-strikeout age in which we live in—count as a hit, an achievement.

"Errors are a nineteenth-century anachronism," Kenny said on air in '18, "and, at this point in baseball, a very subjective call not worth making."

Looking at the data, erasing the error is a compelling idea. As the great sportswriter Joe Posnanski has pointed out, no other sport has anything exactly like the error. If the puck goes off a goalie's glove or foot and into the net, the player who took the shot still gets credit for the goal. When a receiver catches a long pass for a touchdown after the cornerback falls down, we don't rule it an "unearned touchdown." When the shooting guard nails an open look, we don't assign an "E" to the defender who got baited into covering the wrong player.[8]

But at this point, there's no use in litigating the sheer existence of the error in baseball. It's here to stay.

---

8 Though we do assign turnovers, so at least that's something.

What we *can* do is stop assigning deeper meaning to it than it deserves.

Official scorers have a difficult, thankless job. Some of them are colorful characters, like Chicago's Bob Rosenberg, who punctuates every errant throw by a pitcher that allows a baserunner to advance by announcing "WY-ALD PITCH! WY-ALD PITCH" in a high and nasally tone. But we generally only know the names of scorers when they screw up or are thrust into a close call with historic consequences. In that way they are like umpires, albeit with poorer pay and worse sightlines.

These people should serve the purpose of officially documenting the most carefully documented of professional sports, but should not be impacting opinions or paychecks.

And yet, for the longest time, official scorers did exactly that. Errors have an influential duty in the divisor of fielding percentage which, unfortunately, was considered the most reliable measure of defense for decades upon decades.

The examples of Semien and Cordero speak to the big-picture issue with the error, which is that it does not account for a player's defensive range and, by rule, cannot account for mental mistakes or misjudgments (like the one made by Cordero). An inability to even get to a ball that falls in for a hit can positively impact your fielding percentage, while the ability to get a glove on a ball few players would have the athleticism to reach can negatively impact your fielding percentage if it falls in and the official scorer is feeling particularly punitive.

Who is the greatest defensive shortstop of all time? This is a sport capable of driving endless debate and knock-down-drag-out bar brawls if you let it, and yet it would seem a fairly large segment of the fan population would answer in unison, "Ozzie Smith." The Wizard of Oz had a quick release, incredible range, and an acrobatic approach. And yet, among those with at least 1,000 games played at shortstop, Smith's .978 fielding percentage is tied with that of Deivi Cruz for 12th all time. Smith is a percentage point behind Stephen Drew and two points behind Jhonny Peralta. First on the list is Omar Vizquel, with a .985 mark.

Smith's problem is he got to too many balls. He played 21,785 2/3 innings at the position (second only to Derek Jeter) over 19 seasons, made 4,249 putouts (eighth all time), and had 8,375 assists (most all time). His longevity and ridiculous range created more opportunities to make plays . . . and, yes, make errors, which, as we've already explained, are purely subjective. The same play in the same ballpark on different nights might be ruled differently because the scorer on those two nights might be different. Heck, the same scorer could score two identical plays differently depending on the way he was feeling that day (or, say, if he was in a hurry to get home for his wife's birthday).

You might not think a regrettable error decision matters much (that is, unless it affects a no-hitter). But when players are making, at most, 30 to 40 errors in a season (and that's at the very top end), every scoring judgment can impact fielding percentage in a meaningful way. Fielding percentage, after all, is only interested in plays on which a fielder actually touched a ball. Never mind all those balls that might have been fielded had the fielder not moved slowly, misread the ball, or been daydreaming about the post-game dinner spread.

Another issue with the error: It directly impacts a pitcher's Earned Run Average, or ERA. And because ERA is the prevailing means by which many evaluate pitchers, this is indeed a big issue. It adds judgment to the equation of explaining what transpired against a pitcher. (If a pitcher is the one charged with a fielding error that leads to a run, the run is still classified as unearned and doesn't count toward his ERA. Try to figure that one out.)

Fortunately, some smart people realized we need not only better pitcher-evaluation stats (than the standard ERA) but also better defensive stats, like Defensive Runs Saved (DRS) and Ultimate Zone Rating (UZR)—both of which we'll describe in detail in Section 3—which cover all plays and what reasonably could or should be expected of fielders within them.

Again, go back to those two plays from two April nights in 2018: Semien did not make what rated as a fairly difficult play to make. Cordero did not make what rated as a very easy play to make.

Any stat that tells you the first guy failed and then ignores the second guy entirely is, itself, erroneous.

The Err to the Throne

The irony of the error is evident in the case of the all-time record holder for errors, Herman Long. In a 16-year career that began in 1889, Long made 1,096 documented errors. And yet, his contemporaries considered him a standout defender in his day. "Herman Long is the greatest shortstop of them all," Hall of Famer Kid Nichols once said. "You can speak of your [Hughie] Jennings and write of your [Jack] Glasscocks all you want, but this man Long at his best had them beat by a city block."

Long was an early example of a player racking up a high error total because of the range that allowed him to reach those balls in the first place. Alas, his extreme example didn't prevent the error from persisting as an individual evaluation tool in the generations that followed.

WINNING ISN'T EVERYTHING

How the Win Came to Be Baseball's Most Deceptive Pitching Stat

The win stat died—effectively if not officially—on November 14, 2018. It was 134 years old.

Survived by the aura of the "20-game winner," box scores that continue to list Ws and Ls next to pitcher names, and generations of baseball fans blindly bound to the idea of assigning a team achievement to a single individual, the win ultimately succumbed to its inability to keep pace with the changing role of starting pitchers and, well, common sense.

Frail and failing, the win—recorded in modern times by starting pitchers who completed at least five innings and last pitched prior to the half-inning when the winning team took the lead for the last time, or by relief pitchers who recorded the last out before his team took the lead or was judged by the official scorer to be most effective—finally drew its last breath the night of the 2018 National League Cy Young Award announcement. That night, 10-game winner Jacob deGrom of the New York Mets was rightfully and almost unanimously (he fell one vote shy of that standing) selected by the Baseball Writers' Association of America (BBWAA) as the NL's primo pitcher, and the notion of the win as any kind of arbiter of a pitcher's performance was finally, fatally slayed.

The win had been born in 1884 as one of many creations by Henry Chadwick. Widely known as "The Father of Baseball," Chadwick was a pivotal figure in spreading knowledge of the burgeoning sport, and his statistical creations shaped the way team and player performance would be evaluated in the years, decades, and centuries to come. Alas, the win was not his best work. Even in the late 1800s, observers of the game knew better than to take the win seriously. When *The Sporting News* published won-lost records for pitchers for the first time in its July 7, 1888, edition, this was the disclaimer included:

> It seems to place the whole game upon the shoulders of the pitcher and I don't believe it will ever become popular even with so learned a gentleman as Mr. Chadwick to father it. Certain it is that many an execrable pitcher game is won by heavy hitting at the right moment after the pitcher has done his best to lose it.

To repeat: This was written in 1888!

Yet, somehow, the win persevered.

Chadwick first presented the win at a time when free substitutions were not allowed in baseball, meaning pitchers could not leave the game except in the event of injury or if they moved to another position in the field. So the win, as first documented in the 1885 *Spalding Guide*, just went to the pitcher on the winning team. A few years later, Chadwick expanded this concept to losses—with the loss, of course, going to the pitcher on the losing team.

Once substitutions were allowed in 1891, Chadwick tweaked the rule so that the win (or loss) went to the pitcher who threw the most innings in his team's victory (or defeat), a comically unreliable measurement that didn't take the timing of run support into account. In later years, he used different formats to showcase the stat, including listing each pitcher's "Per Cent of Victories" among total games pitched and a rundown of the league's top winners only in games against first-division teams.

Despite the early inconsistencies, the win somehow survived as a meaningful metric in the so-called "modern era," which began with the American League's 1901 claim of major-league status. The *Spalding* and *Reach* guides—the official registers for the National and American Leagues, respectively—included each pitcher's won-lost record. But Chadwick himself tabulated wins and losses for the *Spalding Guide*, without revealing his criteria, and there was no rhyme or reason to how official scorers doled out wins and losses, in general. Many years later, a writer named Frank J. Williams studied box scores from this period and found *eleven different methods* that were used to assign pitcher decisions.

It was calculator chaos.

This confusion resulted in a really strange occurrence at the top of the all-time wins list in the NL. When Grover Cleveland Alexander won his 373rd and final game in 1929 at the age of 42, it was assumed at the time that he had surpassed Christy Mathewson's NL record of 372. But in 1946, somebody went back and did a proper accounting of Mathewson's body of work to find he had been shorted a victory in 1902. The correction was made and, twenty-one years after his death, Mathewson had tied Alexander's mark.

Much like Mathewson, the win forged ahead long after it should have been buried. AL founder Ban Johnson tried to, yes, ban the win as an official stat in 1913, after a kerfuffle over a disputed decision that snapped a long winning streak for Washington Senators hurler Walter Johnson. But Ban's ban caused an uproar from fans and, six years later, the win was back in the *Reach Guide* (it had never left the *Spalding Guide*). By this point, finally, there was more clarity over what a win was, with NL president John Tener decreeing that starting pitchers must pitch at least the first half of a game in order to qualify for the win. By 1918, the win stat as we know it today was more or less in place, though the five-inning minimum for starters would not become official until 1950.

If the concept of the win was fishy when Chadwick invented it, it became frankly farcical when the role of relievers began to rise in the 1950s. A reliever could come into a game and blow the lead the starter left behind but, so long as he was still the active pitcher when his team regained the lead in the next half-inning, he would be credited with the win. Or a starter could conceivably get the first 26 outs of a ballgame and hand it over to a reliever with two outs in the top of the ninth and the game tied. If the reliever got the third out and his team went on to score the winning run in the bottom of the ninth, he—the guy who faced just one batter—would get the win, while the starter would be saddled with a no-decision.[9]

Over the years, fans, writers, managers, and certainly the pitchers themselves came to assign deeper meaning to the win than the stat reasonably deserved. It was not enough to merely succeed in run prevention; you had to also somehow inspire your teammates to produce runs on your behalf. And some truly twisted takes attempted to insist that those who posted gaudy win totals with less-than-stellar run-prevention rates had succeeded in "pitching to the score." They simply "knew how to win" ... even if they didn't always know how to keep the other team from scoring.

This was the argument often used in support of Jack Morris's Hall of Fame case. Morris had a 3.90 ERA for his career, which stretched from 1977 through 1994. But he won 254 games. In fact—and this is really nothing more than trivia, although some used it to support Morris's Hall case—he had more wins in the 1980s than any other pitcher (162).[10] And as a testament to his grit, there was his epic performance in Game Seven of the 1991 World Series, when he threw a 10-inning shutout against the Atlanta Braves to clinch the title for his Minnesota Twins.

---

9 B. J. Ryan (in 2003, with the Baltimore Orioles) and Alan Embree (in 2009, with the Colorado Rockies) were each credited with a victory in a game in which they threw zero pitches. Both relievers picked a runner off a base to end an inning before their offense plated the winning run.

10 Morris was also third in losses in the 1980s, with 119.

Did Morris "pitch to the score?" In other words, did he glide along carelessly in games in which his teams had a big lead and then take his performance to another level when games were close? Baseball analyst Joe Sheehan, then writing for *Baseball Prospectus*, put together "The Jack Morris Project," a game-by-game study of Morris's long career to search for evidence that Morris pitched to the score.

His conclusion?

"I can find no pattern in when Jack Morris allowed runs," Sheehan wrote. "If he pitched to the score—and I don't doubt that he changed his approach—the practice didn't show up in his performance record."

We have numbers to support the notion. The statistical resource site Baseball-Reference.com has splits that divide player performance into high-, medium-, and low-leverage categories (we'll dig into this more in the Win Probability Added chapter in Section 5) based on the score, inning, and the number of baserunners aboard. Morris's opponent numbers (their OPS and OPS+, metrics that we'll cover in Section 2) were virtually identical in those three situations.

But because we haven't covered those statistics yet, let's resort to our old pal batting average's attempt to tell the tale:

> High leverage: .259
> Medium leverage: .246
> Low leverage: .243

That means Morris's opponents had a higher average in the tighter spots, further countering the "pitch to the score" narrative.

So then how did Morris have the most wins in the 1980s? Well, for one, he averaged 35 starts per season for the entirety of the 1980s, which didn't hurt. He also received 4.89 runs of support, on average—the third-most of anybody who pitched all 10 seasons in the '80s. And while Game Seven in 1991 was undoubtedly epic and worthy of consideration in his Hall of Fame bid, his 13-start post-season career resulted in a 3.80 ERA. In other words, in a larger sample of starts, Jack Morris resembled . . . Jack Morris.

Funny how that works.

Morris spent 15 years on the BBWAA ballot and never appeared on more than 67.7 percent of ballots cast in a given year (75 percent is required for entry). But in his first year on the 16-member Modern Era committee ballot, Morris was ushered into the hallowed Hall, along with the highest ERA for an inducted pitcher.

In the interest of full disclosure, I worked with Morris at MLB.com, and had the honor of being there, along with a camera crew, in his hotel suite the night he found out he had achieved entry. I was genuinely happy for Jack and, as a bit of a Big Hall guy myself, I'm not one of those people who are going to decry his induction as a pox on our society.

But did Morris's selection lower the standard for what it takes to be a Hall of Fame starter? Yes, it did. As with his career win total, it was another example of Morris achieving a victory with the support of others.

Morris is far from the only pitcher who benefited from the allure—and illusion—of the win stat. When Commissioner Ford C. Frick announced in 1956 the creation of an annual pitching award named after 511-game winner Cy Young, who had passed away the previous year, the win took on an outsized importance in vote totals for decades to follow.

Where would the appropriately named Early Wynn be without the win in 1959, when he won the Cy Young (then given to just one major-league pitcher, as opposed to one apiece from the AL and NL) on the might of his 22 wins for the Chicago White Sox? Certainly not at the top of the vote totals, because these are the basic credentials voters would have been looking at:

- Early Wynn, Chicago White Sox: 37 games (37 starts), 3.17 ERA, 255 2/3 innings
- Sam Jones, San Francisco Giants: 50 games (35 starts), 2.83 ERA, 270 2/3 innings
- Bob Shaw, Chicago White Sox: 47 games (26 starts), 2.69 ERA, 230 2/3 innings
- Hoyt Wilhelm, Baltimore Orioles: 32 games (27 starts), 2.19 ERA, 226 innings

Looking at that, it would be hard to argue that Wynn's season was more dominant than that of Jones or Wilhelm, who had significantly lower ERAs (and Jones did it in more innings). And if the goal was to reward a member of the White Sox on the heels of their first AL pennant in forty years, then Shaw perhaps deserved equal love to Wynn.

But thanks to that handy little W column, Wynn ran away with the award, garnering 13 out of a possible 16 first-place votes. It was just another win for Wynn.

This pattern repeated itself many times over the years. Let's have some fun with blind bios . . .

1980 American League
Pitcher A: 33 starts, 2.53 ERA, 284 1/3 innings
Pitcher B: 37 starts, 3.23 ERA, 250 2/3 innings
Pitcher C: 36 starts, 2.95 ERA, 283 1/3 innings

Clearly, among the three pitchers listed above, Pitcher A succeeded most in preventing runs, and the fact that he did it in the largest number of innings with the fewest number of starts is a testament to his ability to pitch effectively deep into games.

But Pitcher B (Steve Stone of the Baltimore Orioles) was the Cy Young winner, because he won 25 games. Pitcher A was the Oakland A's Mike Norris, who won 22 games and, to the voters' credit, did garner the same number of first-place votes as Stone, but was low enough on other ballots to finish second overall. I included Pitcher C (the Kansas City Royals' Larry Gura) only as a means of illustrating how much the vaunted 20-win mark mattered in this vote. Gura won 18 games and finished a distant sixth in the Cy Young voting.

Here's another oldie but goodie . . .

1990 American League

Pitcher A: 35 starts, 2.95 ERA, 238 innings

Pitcher B: 36 starts, 2.56 ERA, 267 innings

By now, you're familiar enough with this little game to know that Pitcher A, despite the significantly higher ERA in fewer innings, won the Cy Young. That was 27-game winner Bob Welch of the Oakland A's. But Pitcher B was his own teammate, Oakland ace Dave Stewart, who was arguably more deserving. Alas, Stewart finished third because he "only" won 22 games.

This was just the way things went until the late 2000s/early 2010s, when voter attitudes toward the win evolved enough to grant the 2010 AL Cy Young to Seattle Mariners ace Félix Hernández, despite his 13–12 record.

But it wasn't until Jacob deGrom's unlucky 2018—a season so statistically absurd that it was almost like performance art—that the full fatuousness of the win stat was most evident.

No qualifying pitcher had a better ERA in 2018 than deGrom's 1.70 mark. It was the best in baseball by 0.19 points, and the best in the NL by 0.67. In fact, it was the sixth lowest among qualifying pitchers since the league lowered the mound to its current height in 1969. Furthermore, his 217 innings pitched were the second most in baseball. He set records for consecutive Quality Starts and consecutive starts allowing three or fewer runs.

And he went 10–9.

Jacob deGrom's issue wasn't that he "didn't know how to win." It was that he didn't know how to *not* be on the 2018 New York Mets. They put up 3.57 runs per deGrom start, the third-lowest support average for any qualified pitcher in the majors that season. In the end, deGrom, owner of the league's best ERA (1.70), finished 2018 with the same number of wins as the White Sox's Lucas Giolito, owner of the league's worst ERA (6.13). As the great Jayson Stark wrote of deGrom's Cy Young case in *The Athletic* late in the season, "So are you still asking why we're ignoring wins? It's obvious, isn't it? Because there isn't a single entry on the stat sheet that tells us *less* about how this man has pitched than the entry that most people used to check first. That's why."

All but one of the thirty writers who cast an NL Cy Young vote agreed. And the vote total was all the evidence needed to know that the public at large had finally freed itself from the unnecessary shackles of the win stat.

But that wasn't the only 2018 development that mortally wounded the win. It was also the season that the Tampa Bay Rays unveiled their "opener" strategy, in which a reliever attempts to get the first few outs of the game in a matchup that makes particular sense for him before handing the ball over to a long man or a pitcher who would ordinarily be a starter. As a result, Rays left-hander Ryan Yarbrough was, essentially, a starter who didn't start. He compiled a starter's workload (147 1/3 innings), but the majority of his appearances began in the second, third, or fourth innings. Yarbrough racked up 16 wins despite only having four appearances in which he started a game and worked at least five innings.

The Rays hadn't only reinvented pitching roles, they had hacked the win stat's hard drive and cracked its password.

None of the above prevented the win from continued inclusion on stat pages, baseball cards, and, yes, daily discourse among some fans. So perhaps it is premature to declare the win dead (though you have to admit it made for a compelling lead-in to this section). But in a changing game with improved means of evaluating pitcher performance, it is far too unreliable to be taken seriously.

That was true in 1888, and it is true today.

The Whims (and Wins) of Luck

Lou Gehrig once referred to himself as "The Luckiest Man on the Face of the Earth." But in an altogether different sense, the description might have applied better to left-hander Earl Whitehill, a contemporary of Gehrig's who has the distinction of being credited with more wins (45) in games in which he allowed five earned runs or more than any other pitcher in major-league history.

On the other end of the spectrum, "The Unluckiest Man on the Face of the Earth" might have been Hall of Famer Walter Johnson. Oh, sure, Johnson had a wonderful career as it is, with a win total (417) second only to Cy Young (511). But Johnson also had a whopping 107 games in which he took the loss despite giving up just one earned run. No one else in history has more than 77. With proper support in those games, Johnson would have challenged Young's record—and maybe even had a certain award named after him.

SAVE US FROM THE SAVE

How a Stat with Good Intentions Yielded Bad Results—and Changed the Game Along the Way

Jerome Holtzman would look at the box scores and become incensed.

It was 1959, and a reliever named Roy Face was racking up both wins and praise. Face was a forkball-slinging right-hander for an unspectacular Pittsburgh Pirates team. The Buccos won 78 games that season, and Face was credited with the win in 18 of them.

Not a bad haul for 93 1/3 innings of work across 57 appearances.

Back in 1959, there was really no way to contextualize what Face was accomplishing. The win total drew people in and made them assume that Face was having an extraordinary season. So many writers got sucked into this vortex that Face wound up finishing seventh in the National League MVP voting—ahead of some really good players who had really good years, like future Hall of Famer Frank Robinson and his .311 average, 36 homers, and 125 RBIs (the stats voters would have been paying most attention to at the time) for the Cincinnati Reds.

Holtzman, though, wasn't one of those writers drawn to a pretty Face. An orphan and former marine, he had ascended from copy boy at the *Chicago Daily News* to a baseball writer of renown with the *Chicago Sun-Times* and *The Sporting News*. Holtzman covered a Cubs team that had two relievers—Don Elston and Bill Henry—who he figured must be among the best in baseball. But

Elston and Henry weren't getting nearly as much attention—and ultimately would not garner as much MVP support—as Roy Face.

Having scrutinized the box scores, Holtzman knew the dirty truth about Face: He had allowed the tying or go-ahead run in 10 of his 18 victories. In five of his eventual "wins," he had entered the game with a lead and left without one.

"Everybody thought he was great," Holtzman told *Sports Illustrated* in 1992. "But when a relief pitcher gets a win, that's not good, unless he came into a tie game. Face would come into the eighth inning and give up the tying run. Then Pittsburgh would come back to win in the ninth."

Holtzman knew what we explained earlier in this section: The win stat is a bit of a farce. So he sought to popularize a stat that would specifically demonstrate the effectiveness of relievers. And all these years later, we can say without a shadow of a doubt that Holtzman succeeded in that effort.

Trouble is, the stat he pushed forward isn't any better than the win . . . and has arguably had an even bigger impact on the sport at large.

The save is often credited as Holtzman's invention, but that's not the entire truth. The word "save" had been used to describe a strong effort by a relief pitcher as far back as the early 1900s, and a Brooklyn Dodgers statistician named Allan Roth—a name you'll come across a few times in this book—came up with a template to attach to the word in the early 1950s.

Roth's definition of a save was pretty loose: If a reliever finished off a victory and didn't earn the win, he got the save. It didn't matter if his team won by one run or 10 runs, it was a save all the same.

Holtzman, intent on proving Face's win total was hollow, took Roth's framework and reshaped it to ramp up the requirements of a save, which a reliever could earn one of two ways:

1. By facing the tying or go-ahead run and recording the out in a team victory.
2. By coming into the final inning with a two-run lead and pitching a "perfect" inning (alas, Holtzman did not specify whether a "perfect" inning meant 1-2-3 or merely scoreless).

This is not the save rule we have today. Under Holtzman's rule, a reliever did not have to finish the game to earn a save and, in fact, more than one reliever could qualify for the save in a given game (in those instances, Holtzman reasoned, the official scorer would decide who gets it). Moreover, a reliever could conceivably come in with a four-run lead and the bases empty, allow the opponent to load the bases, and then earn the save by getting out of a jam of his own creation because he had faced the potential tying run.

Despite these quirks—and with Holtzman figuratively shoving the save down people's throats via the pages of *The Sporting News*—the stat began to gain traction. Though the particulars of how a save was calculated varied from club to club, the BBWAA compelled the public relations directors from both leagues to track the save stat during the 1964 season (the NL representatives initially balked at the idea, but eventually caved to public pressure).

The BBWAA went with Holtzman's definition, with one notable addition: A reliever could earn the save by entering with a three-run lead, pitching two or more perfect innings, and finishing the game without giving up the lead.

Though neither league endorsed Holtzman's stat after that 1964 trial run, the save persisted in conversation and media coverage. So, in 1969, the Scoring Rules Committee adopted a simplified version of the save as an official stat: If a reliever entered with a lead, finished with a lead, and could not be credited with a win, he got the save.

This, too, is not the save rule we have today. It was more reflective of the Roth idea, and was far too liberal an application because relievers could earn saves by recording just one out in a blowout victory. Even the relievers themselves scoffed at it—such as in 1973, when Detroit Tigers reliever John Hiller set a record with 38 saves and said, "Some saves are very important. Some are ridiculous."

Thankfully, the Scoring Rules Committee changed the stat in 1974. But they went with something even more ludicrous. For that one season, relievers could earn a save by:

1. Entering a game with the tying or go-ahead run on the bases or at the plate and preserving the lead.
2. Pitching three effective innings while preserving a lead.

Now, as with Holtzman's original rule, you didn't have to finish the game to get the save, and multiple relievers could qualify for the save. And if you pitched three "effective" innings with a 10-run lead, you could earn a save. But if you retired, say, six consecutive batters in the eighth and ninth with a two-run lead, you couldn't.

Uh, yeah . . . that wasn't going to work.

So the Scoring Rules Committee made yet *another* change in 1975, finally bringing us the save rule we have today. To earn the save, a reliever must both finish a game and meet one of the three following conditions:

1. Enter with a lead of no more than three runs and pitch for at least one inning.
2. Enter with the potential tying run either on base, at bat, or on deck.
3. Pitch effectively for at least three innings.

Ultimately, we ended up with a rule quite a bit different from the slightly adapted Holtzman model that was put forward by the BBWAA in 1964. And the biggest difference lies in that first condition. While the 1964 "rule" required pitchers with a three-run lead to work at least two perfect innings, the actual save rule requires only one inning pitched with a three-run lead. That's the condition that fundamentally altered both how relief pitchers were used and how they were paid.

The more the stat became valued in free agency and salary arbitration, the more stock relievers put into being cast into the closer role, and the more managers let that role guide their in-game decision making. No longer were top relievers workhorses in the vein of Face, Elston, and Henry—all of whom pitched north of 90 innings in that aforementioned 1959 season. They were used almost exclusively for one inning, and usually with a lead of no more than three runs. Their roles became hyper-specific, dictated by the stipulations of the save rule and not necessarily by the toughest situation in a game, which can come in an inning earlier than the ninth.

Because of how saves are calculated, we've seen a decline in the number of innings pitched per relief appearance, by decade, from the 1970s through the 2010s:

1970–1979: 1.69
1980–1989: 1.59
1990–1999: 1.24
2000–2009: 1.10
2010–2019: 1.04

In 2017, Hall of Famer Goose Gossage, who averaged more than 100 innings per season in his prime (from 1975–85), lambasted modern-day relief usage—the kind of usage prescribed for

Mariano Rivera en route to his record 652 saves—in a conversation with NJ Advance Media.

> I would like to see these guys come into more jams, into tighter situations and finish the game. In the seventh, eighth, or ninth innings. I don't think they're utilizing these guys to the maximum efficiency and benefit to your ballclub. This is not a knock against Mo, [but] I'd like to know how many of Mo's saves are of one inning with a three-run lead. If everybody in that [bleep]ing bullpen can't save a three-run lead for one inning, they shouldn't even be in the big leagues.

Gossage, whose "old man yells at cloud" interviews became a tired rite of spring in baseball writing circles, was wrong about a lot of stuff—but not this. The save stat had totally changed baseball.

An especially outlandish example of the save being overvalued came in 2014, when the retired relievers who voted for the AL Reliever of the Year Award gave the honor to Kansas City Royals right-hander Greg Holland. To be sure, Holland had a fantastic season—a 1.44 ERA in 62 1/3 innings across 65 appearances, with 90 strikeouts, 20 walks, and a .170 opponents' average. And yes, he also had 46 saves.

But Holland wasn't even the best reliever *on his own team*! That was Wade Davis, who had an even 1.00 ERA in 72 innings across 71 appearances with 109 strikeouts, 23 walks, and a .151 opponents' average. As the setup man, Davis had only three saves. But he was the Royals' most dominant bullpen force and should have won the award.

Thankfully, within the sport, there has been a bit of an awakening when it comes to reliever deployment. Yes, the true workhorses are still rare, and the game had so many relief specialists that MLB instituted a rule beginning with the 2020 season requiring relievers to face at least three batters within an inning or pitch to the end of an half-inning before they are eligible to be replaced by another arm. But it's become more and more common for teams to use their best relievers in non-save situations or to use a committee approach that relies more on the proper matchups in the ninth and less on the so-called "Proven Closer."

A major sea change occurred in the 2016 postseason. That was the year when Baltimore Orioles manager Buck Showalter was roundly ridiculed for leaving Zack Britton, who was on the heels of one of the greatest relief seasons in history (0.54 ERA in 67 innings), sitting on the pine, waiting for a save situation that never arrived in the 11-inning AL Wild Card Game against the Toronto Blue Jays. And it was the same year Cleveland Indians skipper Terry Francona was roundly praised for his aggressive use of uber reliever Andrew Miller as early as the fifth inning in some postseason games. (Guess which team advanced deep into October and which didn't.)

By the winter leading into the 2019 season, the industry had changed so much that Craig Kimbrel—a four-time saves leader, seven-time All-Star, and the active saves leader in baseball—couldn't find a team to meet his price tag in free agency and wound up sitting out half a season before signing with the Cubs for barely half the money (three years, $42 million) that the New York Yankees' Aroldis Chapman and the Los Angeles Dodgers' Kenley Jansen had signed two years earlier.

Front-office executives were no longer willing to pony up humungous price tags for the "Proven Closer," as they knew that the big inning, the big moment, does not always arrive in the ninth. If Reliever A retires the opposition's Nos. 3, 4, and 5 hitters with a one-run lead in the eighth, and Reliever B retires the Nos. 6, 7, and 8 hitters after his team tacks on two insurance runs in the ninth, Reliever B gets the save but Reliever A pitched in the higher-leverage situation.

Still, because the save stat has been around so long and because, for at least a generation, it carried such a strange resonance in the sport, it can be tempting to reflexively turn to it when comparing relief pitchers. Don't fall into that trap. Use stats we'll cover in this book—ERA+, FIP, and WHIP—to evaluate all pitchers, including relievers.

You don't want to let a faulty counting stat trick you into thinking a particular pitcher's season was better than it actually was.

Because isn't that how we ended up with the save stat in the first place?

Saving Grace

If all you knew about Joe Borowski's 2007 season for the Cleveland Indians was that he led the AL in saves, with 45, you would assume he must have been pretty stingy in the realm of run prevention.

But, believe it or not, Borowski had a 5.07 ERA in 65 2/3 innings, with opponents batting .289 against him. In baseball history, he is the only pitcher to save more than 35 games with an ERA over 5.00.

SECTION 2
Batter Up(date)—The Best Offense Stats

Let's begin our deep dive into the advanced metrics—or as I now lovingly refer to them, the "nerdy numbers"—with offensive stats. And obviously "offensive" here means "of or related to offense," not "disrespectful, insulting, or displeasing."

But some fans—even some players, managers, and coaches—have treated the statistics in this section as if the latter definition of offensive applies. Their resistance to change is understandable, on some level. We grew up knowing what a .300 hitter is. We know what that looks like and what that means. We are comfortable with the idea of labeling batters based on their batting average, homer, and RBI output. We heard the story of Boston Red Sox icon Ted Williams staying in the lineup the final day of the 1941 season, when he could have sat on his .39955 average (which would have been rounded up to .400) but instead risked his spot in the history books and, amazingly, went 6-for-8 in the last two games (a doubleheader) to finish at .406.

We didn't know that Williams had also risked losing the first .550 on-base percentage in history, because, well, nobody knew or cared about OBP in 1941.

Some people *still* don't care about it today.

So this section will hopefully demonstrate why you *should* care, and it will help you understand how to use the more modern math to evaluate players. You just might discover these offensive numbers aren't so offensive after all.

OBP (ON-BASE PERCENTAGE)

What it is: *The measure of how frequently a batter reaches base.*

What it is not: *Initials for Orlando Brunson Potter, who helped devise the National Banking Act of 1863.*

How it is calculated: *OBP = Hits + Walks + Hit By Pitch / At Bats[1] + Walks + Hit By Pitch + Sac Flies*

Example: *Willie Mays, OF, 1965 San Francisco Giants*

Hits	Walks	Hit By Pitch	At-Bats	Sacrifice Flies
177	76	0	558	2

177 + 76 + 0 / 558 + 76 + 0 + 2
253 / 636

Willie Mays's 1965 OBP was .398.

Why it matters: *Because, to put it bluntly, outs are bad and not making them is good. And if you believe in the old adage that "a walk is as good as a hit," then OBP is a much more complete measure of a hitter's performance than batting average, which only involves hits per at-bat.*

Where you can find it: *MLB.com, BaseballSavant.com, FanGraphs. com, Baseball-Reference.com, and many other stat resources.*

---

1 Editor's note: We have not included the hyphen in "At-Bats" in each formula that appears in this book, so as to avoid any possible confusion.

We explained earlier why batting average is a flawed statistic. But that doesn't mean it was flawed upon invention.

When our old friend Henry Chadwick unveiled the first box score in 1859 and came up with the concept of batting average not long thereafter, he was actually on to something, given the state of the game he was studying. In a nod to his roots and to baseball's roots, Chadwick had adapted the concept of batting average from cricket's version of the stat. But whereas the cricket measure is runs scored divided by outs, Chadwick correctly noted that, unlike in cricket, runs in baseball are largely dependent on teamwork, not individual skills. So he came up with hits per game, which, in the 1870s, finally evolved into hits per at-bat.

Now, you could say Chadwick had it wrong in using at-bats as opposed to total plate appearances. We must understand, however, that, in the 1860s, walks were relatively rare. Actually, from 1867 to 1887, batters had the right to request a high or low pitch, so you can see why walks were regarded as pitcher mistakes, as opposed to batter achievements. Hitters were judged solely on their ability to make contact, so a rudimentary stat like batting average was applied accurately.

You might have noticed the game is a little bit different today.

The pitfalls of using batting average to assess performance have been present throughout the modern era, but they have been particularly pertinent in the twenty-first century, as Major League Baseball has evolved into a high-power, high-strikeout society. The act—the art, really—of getting on base by any means necessary matters more than ever, and that's why we turn to OBP. The hitter's job, basically, is to avoid making outs. OBP tells us how often the hitter is successful at doing so.

Though it was invented by Brooklyn Dodgers executive Branch Rickey and statistician Allan Roth sometime in the 1940s or 1950s, and became an official MLB statistic in 1984, OBP didn't really have its cultural coming-out party until the 2003 release of

Michael Lewis's *Moneyball: The Art of Winning an Unfair Game.* The book focused on the analytical approach general manager Billy Beane and assistant general manager Paul DePodesta took to assembling the 2002 Oakland A's on a tight budget. Beane believed that power could be developed but patience at the plate and the ability to get on base were more innate. He recognized that OBP had more predictive value than batting average, because OBP ultimately is a product of a player's ability to read pitches, lay off balls and make contact. That's why he targeted an undervalued, low-cost player like Scott Hatteberg (who at that point had a .357 career OBP) in free agency. It was Hatteberg's pinch-hit home run that gave the A's the walk-off win in their then-American League record 20th straight victory in that 2002 season, and served as the climax of the Hollywood adaptation of *Moneyball.*[2]

Moneyball compelled the entire baseball industry—fans, players, and executives alike—to pay greater attention and place greater emphasis on OBP. For many hitters in the present day, it is the stat emphasized above batting average.

"Anytime we're on base," first baseman Yonder Alonso (then with the Cleveland Indians) told me in 2018, "that means the lineup is moving. For me, there's nothing better than being a tough out."

Unlike batting average, OBP involves all of a batter's relevant plate appearances and outcomes. It excludes the sacrifice bunt and catcher's interference; the former is a willing waste of a trip to the plate for the supposed good of the ballclub (although the merits of that play are certainly debatable), and the latter has absolutely nothing to do with a hitter's skill set.

---

2 The 2002 A's also benefited from having three of the best pitchers in baseball in Tim Hudson, Barry Zito, and Mark Mulder, but apparently that didn't make for a compelling enough plot point for Hollywood.

So what is a good OBP? Based on the league average OBP trends over the years, this general rule of thumb, courtesy of FanGraphs, works well:

Rating	OBP
Excellent	.390 or above
Great	.370
Above Average	.340
Average	.320
Below Average	.310
Poor	.300
Awful	.290 or below

Ted Williams once said, "Baseball is the only field of endeavor where a man can succeed three times out of 10 and be considered a good performer." And many a hacky motivational speaker has used that concept to remind us not to be discouraged when we fail.

But Williams was wrong. If a hitter fails seven out of 10 times in his job of not making outs, he has what is described above as a poor OBP. Williams really should have known better, as his .482 career OBP is the highest in history. He "failed" only 52 percent of the time. If anything, those motivational speakers ought to use his example as a means of demonstrating that perhaps we succeed more than we give ourselves credit for.

Speaking of percentages: If OBP has any major flaw, it is presentation. Using the three-digit decimal makes it relatable to those accustomed to the look of batting average, but it would probably be more direct to slide the decimal two places to the right and portray it as a percentage. If your OBP is .350, that means you get on base 35 percent of the time you come to the plate. That's an easy concept to embrace.

One other issue with OBP: The reached-on-error effect. As if the error stat doesn't already have its own issues, when a batter reaches on an error, he is not credited with having gotten on base, even though he quite literally got on base. You can be hit by an errant throw from the pitcher, and your OBP will rise. But if you reach on an errant throw from the shortstop, your OBP actually *drops*.[3]

In any event, Gene Tenace's career is a terrific example of why OBP should be prioritized over BA (batting average).

Fans of a certain age remember Tenace as the 1972 World Series MVP. Fans of a much younger age remember him as the subject of Champ Kind's home run catchphrase in the 2004 comedy *Anchorman: The Legend of Ron Burgundy* ("Gene Tenace at the plate . . . WHAMMY!"). Nobody knows him as a Hall of Famer. Tenace became eligible in 1989 and quickly fell off after appearing on just 0.2 percent of ballots cast. But one wonders if he would have gotten a bit more support in an era in which OBP is a more front-of-mind factor in player evaluation.

For his 15-year career, Tenace hit just .241. But he got on base at an impressive .388 clip—tied with Joe Mauer for the third-highest OBP for a catcher (minimum 3,000 plate appearances) in history. As a matter of fact, in the 10-season span after he became an everyday player in 1973, Tenace posted an OBP of .394. He drew 100 or more walks six times in his career and led his league in walks twice—including the 1974 season, when he hit just .211. He finished with 1,060 hits, yet made 1,075 additional trips to first base via walk or hit by pitch. Even if a modern-day calculation of his credentials still leaves him short of Cooperstown, it might still be fair to refer to Tenace as the right player at the wrong time. In 1980, four years into Tenace's six-year, $1.85 million contract with the San Diego Padres, team owner Ray Kroc was fed up with his catcher.

---

3 Related food for thought: George Brett fell five hits shy of the hallowed .400 batting average in 1980 with the Kansas City Royals. He reached on an error five times that season.

"All he wants to do is walk," Kroc told reporters. "Well, we can't win games waiting for walks. He's being paid to hit, and he can't hit. Nobody in either league wants him, and we're paying a premium price."

Tenace had gotten on base for the Padres in north of 40 percent of his plate appearances. It is impossible to imagine a fair-minded owner or executive saying such things about a player with a .400 OBP today. But for Gene Tenace in 1980, OBP was not enough. The Padres unloaded him to the St. Louis Cardinals in an 11-player trade.

Of course, you'll still occasionally see some old-timers decry OBP. In the 2013 season, the Cincinnati Reds were blessed to have the National League's top two OBPs—Joey Votto at .435 and Shin-Soo Choo at .423—in the top-third of their lineup. It was some kind of irony—or simply proof that the baseball gods have a sense of humor—that their manager was Dusty Baker, who at one point that season told me, "It's not called walking, it's called hitting." Baker was frustrated that Choo and Votto spent too much time at first base and not enough time crossing home plate. But he was missing the point: Choo and Votto were the first set of teammates in the history of baseball's oldest franchise to reach base via hit, walk, or hit by pitch at least 300 times apiece. That was special stuff. Choo and Votto ranked third and fifth, respectively, in runs scored that season, and, sure, it would have been more befitting their contributions to see them ranked first and second in that category, too. But the fact that they weren't was more an indictment of the players who followed them. Choo and Votto had done their job (again, not making outs) and done it exceptionally—even historically—well.

While Baker is right that what goes on at the plate is called hitting, not walking, the sport itself is called *base*ball. So the guys who get on base are indeed valuable.

Down Wit' OBP

Joe DiMaggio's 56-game hitting streak in 1941 is the stuff of baseball legend, in all likelihood never to be repeated. But while DiMaggio got on base at an impressive 46.3-percent clip during that stretch, from May 15 to July 16, Ted Williams bettered him by reaching base in 54 percent of his plate appearances in 55 games across those same dates.

For the season, Williams bettered DiMaggio's OBP by more than 100 points (.553 vs. .440), but the DiMaggio streak mystique weighed supreme in the MVP voting. By the end of this book, if you apply many of the metrics we'll learn about, you'll see that the 1941 MVP case in favor of Williams over DiMaggio is actually overwhelming.[4]

---

4   Much as it pains me, as an Italian American, to admit this.

SLG (SLUGGING PERCENTAGE, OR "SLUG")

What it is: *A measure of a hitter's productivity, with added weight given to extra-base hits.*

What it is not: *A tough-skinned terrestrial mollusk which typically lacks a shell and secretes a film of mucus for protection. Or a slow and lazy person.*

How it is calculated: *SLG = (Singles) + (Doubles x 2) + (Triples x 3) + (Homers x 4) / At Bats, or, put more simply, Total Bases / At Bats*

Example: *Hank Aaron, OF, 1959 Milwaukee Braves*

Singles	Doubles	Triples	Home Runs	At-Bats
131	46	7	39	629

(131) + (46 x 2) + (7 x 3) + (4 x 39) / 629
400 / 629

Hank Aaron's 1959 SLG was .636.

Why it matters: *Because doubles, triples, and home runs are inherently more valuable than singles. Batting average does not account for this difference. Additionally, slugging percentage, as a rate stat, is a better measure of power and production than home runs and RBIs, which are counting stats. It's a better way to compare two players with a dissimilar number of games played.*

Where you can find it: *MLB.com, Baseball Savant, FanGraphs, Baseball Reference, and many other stat resources.*

In incorporating the value of walks, on-base percentage addresses the first flaw that plagues batting average. Slugging percentage handles batting average's other obvious issue, which is its inability to distinguish one type of hit from another.

But let's again be quick to cut batting average inventor Henry Chadwick some slack. For one, before he even put forth batting average, Chadwick stumbled upon what can best be described as a prehistoric version of slugging percentage when he proposed a statistic in which total bases were divided by games. Change the denominator from games to at-bats, and you have slugging percentage, which would become an official stat in the National League in 1923 and the American League in 1946.

So, if Chadwick understood the importance of total bases, why did he give us a batting average statistic in which all hits are (wrongly) created equal?

The answer is that, in Chadwick's time, fielders were terrible! And it sure didn't help that their gloves were basically form-fitting leather covers meant more for hand protection than fielding assistance.[5] So it was not easy to distinguish an error from a misplay and, ergo, not easy to distinguish an earned extra-base hit from one that was the gift of some fielding foible. As relayed by official MLB historian John Thorn in his *Our Game* blog (ourgame. mlblogs.com), this is what Chadwick wrote in his article "The True Test of Batting" in the September 19, 1867, edition of *The Ball Players' Chronicle*:

> Our plan of adding to the score of outs and runs the number of times—not the number of bases—bases are

---

5 The idea for the webbing in gloves did not arrive until 1919.

made on clean hits will be found the only fair and correct test of batting; and the reason is, that there can be no mistake about the question of a batsman's making his first base, that is, whether by effective batting, or by errors in the field, such as muffing a ball, dropping a fly ball, or throwing badly to the bases, whereas a man may reach his second or third base, or even get home, through errors of judgment in the out-field in throwing the ball to the wrong man, or in not properly estimating the height of the ball, etc.—errors which do not come under the same category as those by which a batsman makes his first base.

That was a long-winded, old-fashioned way of saying batting average was the best they could do at the time.

We've already discussed the fact that erroneous error counts still have an unfortunate effect on modern-day statistics, but we can feel far better about the legitimacy of doubles, triples, and home runs today than we could have in the 1800s. So slugging percentage takes on the important task of telling us more about what type of hits a player is producing.

To be sure, SLG has imperfections of its own. Like batting average, it leaves out walks, so it's not going to tell you everything you need to know about a hitter. And if you want to pick nits, in the context of scoring runs, it's not always true that a double is worth exactly twice as much as a single, but SLG calculates it that way.

Still, SLG is one of the best evaluators of power in baseball, because it accounts for more than just home runs.

League-wide SLG trends can vary widely from era to era, so it's a little more difficult to assign ratings to SLG marks than OBP marks (that's why league-adjusted context stats are so important, and we'll cover those in later chapters). For instance, in the 50-season span from 1970 to 2019, the league-average OBP was anywhere from .311 to .345, a range of 34 points. But the league-wide SLG was anywhere from .354 to .437, a range of 83 points. How we judge SLG can also be tied to a player's position. Certainly, if your club is going to carry a defensive liability at first base, he'd better have a good SLG. But if you've got a defensive whiz at shortstop, it's more acceptable if his SLG is substandard.

With all that said, a rough rundown of how to gauge a given player's SLG in the present day would look something like this:

Rating	SLG
Excellent	.550 or above
Great	.500
Above Average	.450
Average	.420
Below Average	.400
Poor	.390
Awful	.380 or below

Of course, some all-time greats weren't exactly sultans of SLG. Tony Gwynn only had four .500 SLG marks among his 20 seasons. Wade Boggs and Pete Rose only had one apiece. Ichiro Suzuki, that famous slapper of infield singles, had a career SLG of .402. Ozzie Smith had a higher career OBP (.337) than SLG (.328). We don't judge these players on the SLG stat, because pure power was not integral to their style or their game.[6]

SLG is really best used to identify where a hitter's current power production stands in relation to his career trend or what's

---

6 For the record, no player has finished his career with a perfect 4.000 SLG (in other words, homered in his only career at-bat or at-bats). But catcher Charlie Lindstrom of the 1958 Chicago White Sox is the only position player to triple in his lone at-bat, giving him a 3.000 SLG for his career.

going on around the league. In this century, baseball has seen a significant rise in the number of strikeouts. This has created an even wider discrepancy in the overall value of SLG vs. BA, because with fewer balls in play, the damage done on balls in play takes on added importance.

Take these two players from the 2017 Colorado Rockies as an example of the significance of SLG:

Player	BA	OBP	SLG
DJ LeMahieu	.310	.374	.409
Nolan Arenado	.309	.373	.586

Two infielders, two good defenders, two key contributors to the Rockies' claim of a wild-card spot in the postseason, two darn-near-identical averages and on-base percentages. But which guy got MVP votes and a $17.75 million salary in arbitration the following winter?

Right, that would be Arenado.

SLG can help us understand when a player has managed to produce power without an eye-catching home run total, and it can also help us understand when a player's gaudy home run total is actually somewhat hollow. For example, in 2017, Texas Rangers second baseman Rougned Odor hit 30 home runs, but his SLG was only .397. He was plagued by pop-ups that season, didn't draw many walks, and, despite the impressive homer total, actually recorded 16 fewer extra-base hits than he had a year earlier, despite playing in 12 more games.

Juxtapose Odor's odd season with Rod Carew's MVP output for the Minnesota Twins in 1977. Carew hit just 14 homers that year, but his SLG was .570 because he hit 38 doubles and an American League–leading 16 triples. Carew was proof that you don't have to hit the ball out of the park to have an MVP-caliber SLG.

So SLG serves a worthwhile purpose as OBP's weight-lifting, protein shake–drinking cousin. And their family get-togethers provide us with a batting average–besting stat known as OPS, which we'll cover next.

What's My Line?

If you ever see a reference to "slash" and you are reading a baseball article and not a discussion about the guitarist for the rock band Guns N' Roses, then it is probably referring to a ballplayer's "slash line" (sometimes referred to as a "triple-slash"). That, in order, is his batting average, on-base percentage, and slugging percentage.

For instance, in 1988, Cleveland Indians outfielder Cory Snyder[7] had a .272 BA, .326 OBP, and .483 SLG, so his triple-slash line would be written as .272/.326/.483. In baseball writing, this is used as a quick way to relay a player's offensive contributions and is preferable to the old-school usage of batting average, home runs, and RBIs, because it tells us more.

---

7 I know it's a random reference, but Snyder was my favorite player as a kid, so I had to sneak him in this book somewhere.

OPS (ON-BASE PLUS SLUGGING)

What it is: *A measure of a player's ability to get on base and hit for power.*

What it is not: *The short, hip way to say "operations" or "opposites."*

How it is calculated: $OPS = OBP + SLG$

Example: *Roberto Clemente, OF, 1967 Pittsburgh Pirates*

OBP	SLG
.400	.554

.400 + .554

Roberto Clemente's 1967 OPS was .954.

Why it matters: *Because convenience reigns supreme, and statisticians realized we needed a single go-to number to evaluate hitters that was better than batting average.*

Where you can find it: *MLB.com, Baseball Savant, FanGraphs, Baseball Reference, and many other stat resources.*

If you've ever put peanut butter on a hamburger, if you've ever drizzled olive oil over vanilla ice cream, if you've ever used Coca-Cola as a steak marinade, if you've ever dipped your Wendy's french fries into a Frosty, you know that two edible items—seemingly independent in their awesomeness—can sometimes pair surprisingly well together.[8]

OPS is akin to the above offerings in that curiosity compelled somebody to take two disparate numbers—each intriguing enough on its own—and just mash them together in a sort of statistical sandwich. First popularized in 1984 by John Thorn and Pete Palmer's book *The Hidden Game of Baseball*, and spread by the great Peter Gammons and other baseball writers in the 1990s, OPS finally wound its way into our Topps baseball cards and daily discourse in the 2000s.

It is a stat that is both complex and crude. Actually, OPS is mathematically problematic. Remember: On-base percentage uses plate appearances as its denominator, while slugging percentage uses at-bats. Back in school, we learned that you can't add two fractions with unlike denominators. If they are unlike, before you can add the fractions, you must find the least common multiple of the two denominators and ... well, I forget the rest, because that's where I started to zone out and daydream about baseball.

The creators of OPS didn't worry about such math maxims. They just slapped two pieces of bread around OBP and SLG and dug into some delectable batter data. God bless 'em.

OPS tells us how well a player gets on base and how well he hits for power. Now, while it has some major flaws in relaying that information (we'll get into those in just a sec), it's still a major step forward from batting average and RBIs.

This is the FanGraphs-recommended approach to evaluating hitters based on their OPS:

---

8 Back in college, I had a summer job painting houses with a guy who lived by the questionable—but also delightfully straightforward—mantra that, in his words, "Anything good tastes good with anything good." It wasn't a foolproof principle, but he was correct a lot more often than you'd think.

Rating	OPS
Excellent	1.000
Great	.900
Above Average	.800
Average	.700
Below average	.670
Poor	.600
Awful	.570

Only seven players with at least 3,000 plate appearances have logged a career OPS of 1.000 or higher: Rogers Hornsby (1.010), Hank Greenberg (1.017), Jimmie Foxx (1.038), Barry Bonds (1.051), Lou Gehrig (1.080), Ted Williams (1.116), and Babe Ruth (1.164). The average OPS for a Hall of Famer, as of this writing, is .841, which was actually the exact career mark of both Cap Anson and Carl Yastrzemski.

Thanks to OPS, there was no great mystery as to which of these players had the superior offensive season in 2014:

Player, Team	BA	OBP	SLG	OPS
Ben Revere, PHI Phillies	.306	.325	.361	.686
Edwin Encarnación, TOR Blue Jays	.268	.354	.547	.901

Encarnación didn't hit .300? Who cares? He got on base, and he raked.

OPS works best as an evaluator of team offense, because it correlates really well with runs scored. How well? If we determine the correlation coefficient—in which 1 is a perfect positive correlation and 0 is no correlation at all—to 10 seasons of team-by-team offensive data from 2009 to 2018, these are the correlations between specific stats and team runs per game:

BA: 0.689
OBP: 0.841
SLG: 0.906
OPS: 0.947

So OPS has great utility in assessing a team's offensive performance.

Of course, in solving the problem of batting average, OPS creates another issue (or OPS-tacle?) with its own formulaic imperfections.

As we discussed previously, the highest possible SLG is 4.000, while the highest possible OBP is 1.000. When combining these two numbers, the majority of input and impact is going to come from the SLG side of things. But because of the smaller possible range, one point of OBP is worth more than one point of SLG.[9] So OPS is probably guilty of overrating power hitters and underrating high on-base players.

OPS also doesn't adjust for hitting environments. Todd Helton played a career's worth of home games in the high-altitude (and high run total) environment of Colorado's Coors Field, and had a 1.048 OPS in 4,841 plate appearances in that building vs. an .855 OPS in 4,612 plate appearances elsewhere. That .855 OPS on the road is still pretty darn good, but the stark split between home and road means we have to affix Helton's .953 career OPS—a mark that ranks in the top 20 all time among those with at least 3,000 career plate appearances—with a Rocky Mountain–sized qualifier.

But OPS is still worlds better than batting average. And though there are other offensive numbers that do a better job providing context and don't have the formulaic flaws that OPS

---

9   For what it's worth, Tom Tango, the Senior Database Architect of Stats for MLB Advanced Media, has theorized that OBP is nearly two times more valuable than SLG, in terms of driving offensive success.

possesses (we'll get into those in later chapters), OPS has already succeeded in finding its place on jumbotrons and in regular baseball dialogue, which is half the battle.

It might not fill you up as much as a peanut butter burger, but it's a fairly satisfying stat.

OPS Attracts

We think of Babe Ruth as the dominant home run hitter of his time, the so-called "Sultan of Swat." The term "Emperor of OPS" would have applied just as well, if not better. Ruth led the AL in home runs a record 12 times during his legendary career. But he led the league in OPS a whopping 13 times, also the most ever. He led the American League in OPS every year from 1918 to 1931, except 1925; that mysterious season in which Ruth was plagued by what was known as "the bellyache heard 'round the world." (He still had a .936 OPS in 98 games.)

RC (RUNS CREATED)

What it is: *An estimate of a player's total offensive contribution to his team in terms of total runs.*

What it is not: *A type of cola.*

How it is calculated: *RC = (Hits + Walks + Hit By Pitch - Caught Stealing - Grounded Into Double Play) x (Total Bases + .26[Walks - Intentional Walks + Hit By Pitch]) + (.52[Sacrifice Hits + Sacrifice Flies + Stolen Bases]) / (At Bats + Walks + Hit By Pitches + Sacrifice Hits + Sacrifice Flies)*

> **Note:** The .26 and .52 are weights Runs Created creator Bill James gave to walks, hit batsmen, sacrifices, and stolen bases on their relation to potential runs scored.

Example: *Ryne Sandberg, 2B, 1984 Chicago Cubs*

Hits	At-Bats	Walks	Intentional Walks	Hit By Pitch
200	636	52	3	3

Stolen Bases	Caught Stealing	Grounded Into Double Play
32	7	7

Sacrifice Hits	Sacrifice Fly	Total Bases
5	4	331

(200 + 52 + 3 - 7 - 7) x (331 + .26[52 - 3 + 3]) + (.52[5 + 4 + 32]) / (636 + 52 + 3 + 5 + 4)

88167.44 / 700

Ryne Sandberg's 1984 RC was 126.

Why it matters: *Because the central job of a hitter is to help his team score runs, and this is a better means than RBIs or runs scored for evaluating how well the hitter completed that task in a given season.*

Where you can find it: *FanGraphs and Baseball Reference.*

Bill James is often referred to as the "godfather of sabermetrics," and many have advocated that his profound influence on the sport be celebrated with induction into the National Baseball Hall of Fame.

But back in the late 1970s, he was just a night shift security guard at a Stokely-Van Camp's cannery.

Evidently, there weren't many attempts by thieves to pilfer pork and beans, because James had plenty of spare time to write provocative—sometimes contentious—baseball articles that compelled his readers to see the game a different way. Usually, these articles began with a very simple premise, such as, "Which pitchers and catchers allow the most stolen bases?" And then, in an inimitable style awash with wit, James would find the answers to his questions in bold and fresh new ways.

That technique was especially effective—and influential—when James came up with Runs Created, which, if you're scoring at home, gives him one Runs Created created.

The question behind this stat is simple and straightforward. This is what James wrote in *The Bill James Historical Baseball Abstract*, published in 1985:

> With regard to an offensive player, the first key question is how many runs have resulted from what he has done with

the bat and on the basepaths. Willie McCovey hit .270 in his career, with 353 doubles, 46 triples, 521 home runs and 1,345 walks—but his job was not to hit doubles, nor to hit singles, nor to hit triples, nor to draw walks or even hit home runs, but rather to put runs on the scoreboard. How many runs resulted from all of these things?

Here's the original formula James proposed to answer that question: Total Bases x (Hits + Walks) / (At Bats + Walks)

Pretty simple. Combine a player's ability to get on base with his ability to advance on the bases and divide those two by his total opportunities.

That was the formula James introduced in 1979. In the ensuing years, he tweaked it many times to account for stolen bases, to adjust the weights given to certain numbers, to adjust for eras, etc. I could take you through all of these adjustments. I could cite the 13 (yes, 13) different technical versions of RC that John Thorn and Pete Palmer introduced in their 1989 book, *Total Baseball*. I could walk you through the further advancements pushed forward by James and others in the 1990s and 2000s, when lineup position and other factors were taken into account. And there are several other stats that fall into the category of "run estimators"— including Palmer's "Linear Weights," Jim Furtado's "Extrapolated Runs," and David Smyth's "Base Runs"—that do as good as or even a better job than RC.

But look, I promised you this book wouldn't be weighed down by too much mathematical mumbo jumbo and extraneous analytics. We're here to focus on what's embraceable, relatable, and easily accessible. Understanding the concept of RC is important because it contributes to our understanding of Weighted Runs Created Plus, which, for my money, is the best offensive metric readily available today (and will be covered later in this section). And as far as the specific RC formula, what is cited above is officially known as the "technical version" of RC. It's the formula used by Baseball Reference on its stats pages (for all seasons that include stolen base and caught stealing data), and is therefore the formula likely to have been used whenever you see a player's RC total cited in the media.

Because RC—much like HRs and RBIs—is a counting stat and not a rate stat, players who miss time due to injury or other factors are going to have their RC totals affected. So there would be little value to establishing a rating system for RC as we have with many other stats in this book, because how we view a player's RC mark is ultimately going to be dependent on the run-scoring environment from year to year. For instance, in 1965, the Cleveland Indians' Rocky Colavito led the American League in RC with 110. In 2000, there were 28 AL players who had a RC mark at least that high, and the leader (the Toronto Blue Jays' Carlos Delgado) had an RC of 186.

Where this stat works best is in the comparing of players within a single season. Consider this example from the 1958 season:

Player, Team	Runs	HRs	RBIs	RC
Ernie Banks, Chicago Cubs	119	47	129	135
Willie Mays, San Francisco Giants	121	29	96	152

Again, this was 1958, long before anybody was thinking about RC or context stats. Banks dominated in the home run and RBI totals, and he dominated in the MVP voting (the vote wasn't related to team performance, for Banks's Cubs lost eight more games than Mays's Giants). Banks received 16 first-place votes to Mays's three. But because of the added offensive value Mays had contributed in getting on base (78 walks to Banks's 52) and stealing bases (31 to Banks's four), he provided 17 more RC and, arguably, had the superior offensive season.[10]

If you want to use RC as a rate and not just a counting number, RC27 is available on some stats pages, such as the ones provided by ESPN and FOX Sports. This stat multiplies the denominator in the RC calculation by 27 to determine how many runs a lineup of nine of the same player would average per nine-inning game (or 27 outs). It's imprecise, to be sure, but at least it's useful in understanding the relative pace of production for players who are part-timers or miss a lot of games due to injury.

So when Boston Red Sox designated hitter David Ortiz was limited by an Achilles injury to 90 games and 383 plate appearances in 2012, it affected his RC total. But in that smallish sample, Ortiz had a RC27 of 9.2, which was higher than that of 2012's overall RC leader Miguel Cabrera, who had a 134 RC and 8.0 RC27. A full lineup of healthy David Ortizes would have scored north of nine runs per game.

Just don't ask how that lineup would have fared on defense, OK?

---

10 This wasn't the only time Mays would have been deserving of the MVP Award but didn't win. We'll demonstrate in a later chapter how modern metrics make it clear Mays was hosed multiple times in the voting.

Fun Created

There have only been ten instances in which a player has logged an RC mark of 200 or more in a single season:

1. 230: Barry Bonds, 2001 San Francisco Giants
2. 229: Babe Ruth, 1921 New York Yankees
3. 209: Babe Ruth, 1923 New York Yankees
4. 208: Lou Gehrig, 1927 New York Yankees
5. 208: Barry Bonds, 2002 San Francisco Giants
6. 203: Barry Bonds, 2004 San Francisco Giants
7. 202: Rogers Hornsby, 1922 St. Louis Cardinals
8. 202: Jimmie Foxx, 1932 Philadelphia Athletics
9. 201: Babe Ruth, 1927 New York Yankees
10. 200: Babe Ruth, 1920 New York Yankees

ISO (ISOLATED POWER)

What it is: *A measure of the raw power of a hitter.*

What it is not: *An acronym for "In Search Of . . ." used when you're looking to buy something on Craigslist.*

How it is calculated: *ISO = SLG - BA*

Example: *Ken Griffey Jr., OF, 1997 Seattle Mariners*

SLG	Average
.646	.304

.646 - .304

Ken Griffey's 1997 ISO was .342.

Why it matters: *Because batting average does not tell you how often a player's hits go for extra bases, and slugging percentage does not discriminate between singles and extra-base hits. ISO shows us which hitters have extra-base power.*

Where you can find it: *Baseball Savant, Baseball Reference, and FanGraphs.*

In the formulaic food chain that accompanies the increased statistical sophistication over the past few years, ISO is an obvious and necessary step forward from SLG, though it is not as widely cited (yet).

Still, ISO is a useful tool, and one that actually has roots dating all the way back to the aforementioned Branch Rickey and

Allan Roth. Later in this book, in the chapter on Run Differential, we'll delve into a 1954 article from *Life* magazine in which Rickey put forth a formula that expressed and stressed the importance of a team scoring more runs than it allows over the course of a season. But one small element of that formula concerned what Rickey referred to as "Extra-Base Power."

"There are several ways of computing this," Rickey wrote. "The conventional slugging average which most baseball people use is simply total bases over times at bat. My own formula for computing power, which I have used for years, and called 'isolated power,' is the number of extra bases over and above singles in relation to total number of hits. It turns out that neither of these is as reliable in determining extra base power as a formula which combines the two."

Rickey, using a formula created by Roth, proposed:

(Total Bases - Hits) / Times At Bat

That's just another way of expressing the same, more readily memorable SLG minus BA equation listed above. So way back in 1954, Rickey understood that SLG could mask a player's power when that player does not hit for a high average.

Because it is not adjusted for run-scoring environments, the league average ISO will fluctuate from season to season. But here's the FanGraphs rule of thumb for ISO:

Rating	ISO
Excellent	.250
Great	.200
Above Average	.170
Average	.140
Below Average	.120
Poor	.100
Awful	.080

Three players with a minimum of 3,000 plate appearances finished their careers with ISO marks north of .300: Babe Ruth (.348), Mark McGwire (.325), and Barry Bonds (.309). Bonds's .536 mark from 2001 is the all-time highest single-season ISO.

If you put particular value in a player's power—say, when deciding who to draft in your fantasy league—ISO is a nice next step to turn to when comparing two players with similar SLG marks. If a player has a major jump in SLG from one year to the next, be sure to investigate his ISO as well, because a high average emanating from a high rate of singles can artificially inflate his SLG.

Here's an example of a situation in which ISO had predictive power: In 2006, a 32-year-old Derek Jeter finished second in the AL MVP voting after logging a .343 average with 14 homers, 39 doubles, and 97 RBIs for the New York Yankees. Meanwhile, a 22-year-old Hanley Ramírez won the NL Rookie of the Year with a .292 average, 17 homers, 46 doubles, and 59 RBIs for the Florida Marlins.

The two shortstops had similar SLG marks, but there was a 48-point difference in their ISOs:

Player	SLG	ISO
Jeter	.483	.140
Ramírez	.480	.188

Beyond the decade difference in their ages, it was pretty clear which player was more likely to maintain a strong power presence moving forward.

Sure enough, over the next three seasons (2007–09), the numbers looked like this:

Player	SLG	ISO
Jeter	.442	.131
Ramírez	.549	.239

ISO won't always function as a predictor of future power performance, and it doesn't serve as a replacement for OPS or some of the other catch-all metrics we will discuss in future chapters. So it doesn't always work in . . . ISOlation. But in telling us which share of a player's hits go for extra bases, it adds context to SLG and helps you determine what kind of hitter you are assessing.

ISO Facto

In 2017, the Texas Rangers' Joey Gallo posted the lowest batting average (.209) for a player with an ISO of .300 or more (.327). That's because Gallo became just the third player in history (joining Bonds and McGwire) to qualify for the batting title while hitting more homers (41) than singles (32).

wOBA (WEIGHTED ON-BASE AVERAGE)

What it is: *A version of on-base percentage that accounts for not just whether a player reached base, but how he reached base.*

What it is not: *A radio station's call letters.*

How it is calculated: *wOBA = (.69 x Unintentional Walks) + (.72 x Hit By Pitch) + (.88 x Singles) + (1.25 x Doubles) + (1.58 x Triples) + (2.03 x Homers) / At Bats + Walks - Intentional Walks + Sacrifice Flies + Hit By Pitch*

> **Note:** The numbers used above (.69, .72, .88, etc.) fluctuate slightly from year to year based on each event's (walk, hit by pitch, single, double, triple, homer) relation to projected runs scored in that given season. What is presented here is a representative sample from the 2018 season, which we will also use in the example. At the FanGraphs site, you can peruse the different "weights" used for each season.

Example: *Mookie Betts, OF, 2018 Boston Red Sox*

Singles	*Doubles*	*Triples*	*Home Runs*	*At-Bats*
96	47	5	32	520

Walks	*Intentional Walks*	*Sacrifice Flies*	*Hit By Pitch*
81	8	5	8

(.69 x 73) + (.72 x 8) + (.88 x 96) + (1.25 x 47) + (1.58 x 5) + (2.03 x 32) / 520 + 81 - 8 + 5 + 8

50.37 + 5.76 + 84.48 + 58.75 + 7.9 + 64.96

272.22 / 606

Mookie Betts's 2018 wOBA was .449.

Why it matters: *Because not all methods of reaching base are equal. OBP only goes so far in measuring offensive value, whereas wOBA assigns the proper value to each event in terms of its impact on scoring runs.*

Where you can find it: *FanGraphs and Baseball Savant.*

Let's just get right to the heart of the matter here. Even if this stat is not for you, even if you find the formula too complicated, even if you would rather just focus on the easier-to-understand OBP, you do have to admit this much:

wOBA is fun to say.

Assuming we can agree that the proper pronunciation is "whoa-bah," then I think we can also agree on that point. And if we can agree on that point, then we can take the next, natural step and agree that the best way to describe a player who has a phenomenal wOBA would be to say, "He puts the 'whoa' in wOBA!"

With that vital conversation out of the way, let's dig into this stat's origins and importance.

wOBA was created by Tom Tango, a statistician who has worked and consulted with several teams and who now serves as Senior Database Architect of Stats for MLB Advanced Media. Back in 2006, Tango (the name is actually an alias, as "Tom Tango" has opted to keep his real name private) helped write *The Book* on sabermetrics. Literally, that's what it was called: *The Book: Playing the Percentages in Baseball.* Co-written with Mitchel Lichtman and Andrew Dolphin, *The Book* used cold, hard, emotionless data to propose statistical arguments for how best to optimize a lineup, manage a game, etc.

The wOBA stat was a product of *The Book*. It was a step forward from OBP or OPS because it put the appropriate weight on the various means of reaching base. Tango didn't pluck these weights out of thin air. They come from actual data from a given year of how these events impacted run-scoring.

As you can see from the weights in the formula, a walk is not necessarily as good as a hit, because a hit can advance the runners further. Historically, hit by pitches have been shown to be more valuable than walks, perhaps because even some unintentional walks are, in fact, intended as means of setting up double plays or bringing a lesser batter to the plate. Whatever the reason, what is clear is that a double is more valuable than (but not worth twice as much as) a single, a triple more valuable than a double, and a homer more valuable than a triple.

wOBA accounts for all of this. So at the risk of bogging you down with yet another formula, the math looks like this: BA < OBP < wOBA.

The wOBA stat is also a step forward from OPS because of those aforementioned issues that come with combining on-base percentage and slugging percentage into a single metric. Namely, the OPS formula wrongly assumes that OBP and SLG have similar values when, in fact, the results show that OBP is the more valuable number of the two when it comes to producing runs.

Now that I've explained the formula, let's answer the big question: What's a good wOBA?

The good news here is that, to make this all easier to comprehend, wOBA's formula has been scaled to resemble OBP. Therefore, we can resurrect the OBP rules of thumb and apply it to wOBA:

Rating	wOBA
Excellent	.390 or above
Great	.370
Above Average	.340
Average	.320
Below Average	.310
Poor	.300
Awful	.290 or below

And as we noted in the formula, different years come with different weights. Take Ted Williams's 1951 season with the Boston Red Sox and Edgar Martínez's 1996 season with the Seattle Mariners as an example. Both players put up a .464 OBP those years. Martínez, however, had the higher SLG, and, ergo, the higher OPS—1.059 to Williams's 1.019. So Edgar had the better offensive year, right?

Well, not necessarily. Because of differences in the parks, the pitching, and any number of additional factors, getting on base carried a greater weight in 1951 than it did in 1996. Look at the differences in inputs for the wOBA formula for these two seasons:

Season	BB	HBP	1B	2B	3B	HR
1951	.732	.764	.930	1.314	1.660	2.128
1996	.719	.748	.901	1.252	1.568	1.975

The same events were worth less in Martínez's time than in Williams's time. And that's what wOBA is all about: Giving events their proper value.

Well . . . that, and being fun to say.

Know-ba your wOBA

In case you needed yet another means of demonstrating that Babe Ruth was good at baseball, know this: He's the only player in history with a career wOBA over .500 (.513). Go ahead and say it with me now: "He puts the 'whoa' in wOBA!"

wRC+ (WEIGHTED RUNS CREATED PLUS) AND OPS+ (ON-BASE PLUS SLUGGING PLUS)

What they are: *Versions of Runs Created and OPS that normalize the stats by accounting for important external factors like ballpark and era.*

What they are not: *Versions of Runs Created and OPS that are fortified with extra vitamins and minerals.*

How they are calculated: *wRC+ = (((([wOBA - league wOBA / wOBA scale] x Plate Appearances) + league Runs / Plate Appearances) + (league Runs per Plate Appearance - Park Factor x League Runs per Plate Appearance)) / (AL or NL wRC per Plate Appearance, excluding pitchers))) x 100*
OPS+ = (OPS / league OPS, adjusted for park factors) x 100

> **Note:** The run environment changes year to year, which means the exact numbers used in these formulas (ballpark factor, league runs per PA, etc.) change from year to year. And because all of this is super complicated and it's hard to even envision a scenario in which you have the need to calculate these by hand, we're going to skip the example here.

Why they matter: *Because while Runs Created and OPS were both huge steps forward from more antiquated offensive metrics, neither* *one is adjusted for the context of a given season or a player's home park. The "plus" versions of these stats help us not only compare players within the snapshot of a season but also across eras.*

Where you can find it: *wRC+ is at FanGraphs, and OPS+ is at Baseball Reference.*

These are different stats, calculated in different ways. But I have opted to group them together in this chapter because they are two variations of the same idea, which is to tell us where a player's offensive production stands in relation to the league average.

To be clear, wRC+ is a step forward from OPS+ in terms of its inputs, so it has the honor and privilege of being listed first here. Way to go, wRC+!

But here's the rub: wRC+ marks are most easily accessible at FanGraphs, and OPS+ marks are most easily accessible at Baseball Reference. Neither is available at the other site, and the fact is that certain people are going to gravitate toward certain stat pages. Actually, if you Google the name of a player—any player—right now, his Baseball Reference page is likely to be one of the first links provided. So while wRC+ might be ahead of OPS+ in terms of what it tells us about a player, it is behind OPS+ in the perhaps-equally-important realm of search engine optimization.

Having sufficiently explained (I hope) why these stats are sharing a chapter, let's go over what to make of them.

The first thing that must be understood to fully appreciate either of these stats is the value of "average." In many contexts, "average" is unfulfilling and uninteresting. If you described a first date, a meal, or a movie as "average," it would not exactly be a glowing review. When Joe Walsh wrote "Ordinary Average Guy," he was deliberately attempting to demystify the legend of the modern rock star and remind people that, even if you occasionally play screaming guitar solos for the adoring masses, you still have to pick up your dog's manure off the sidewalk. There was no glory in "average."[11]

But in Major League Baseball, average—the description, not the stat—ain't necessarily bad. Heck, some of the most essential players on the modern roster are the guys who can play multiple defensive positions (or just one at an elite level) while providing league average numbers at the plate. While players with huge contracts or outsized offensive expectations will of course want to do better than produce at a rate commensurate with the league average, for many players such production will keep you gainfully employed.[12]

What wRC+ and OPS+ both do is scale "league average" to 100. A player with a wRC+ or OPS+ of 110 is 10 percent better than the league average offensively. A player with a wRC+ or OPS+ of 90 is 10 percent worse than league average offensively. Go ahead and accuse the calculation—maybe even the concept— of these two stats being difficult for the common fan to understand, but the end result is actually pretty simple.

Here's the FanGraphs rule of thumb for how to evaluate a player using both of these stats:

Rating	wRC+ or OPS+
Excellent	160
Great	140
Above Average	115
Average	100
Below Average	80
Poor	75
Awful	60

11 As if to emphasize the point, the AllMusic.com review of the *Ordinary Average Guy* album gives it just two stars out of five, which is below average.

12 And if you can obtain the average big-league salary, which in recent seasons has been north of $4 million, you can probably afford to pay somebody else to pick up your dog's poop.

Babe Ruth is the all-time career in both wRC+ (195) and OPS+ (206), so the stats pass the smell test.

Remember when we referenced Joey Votto's 2013 season when discussing OBP? After that season, he was asked by Cincinnati radio station ESPN 1530 for his favorite offensive stat. His answer was wRC+.

"I'm all about keeping things fair," Votto said, "and evaluating a player based on what he does all around."

Votto had driven in just 73 runs the previous season, creating consternation among fans and his manager, who desired more from the $225 million man. Votto was routinely ripped on the radio airwaves that year by people who felt he was too concerned with drawing walks and not driving in runs or launching long balls.

But when you look at the wRC+ leaderboard from 2013, you understand why Votto valued the stat:

1. Miguel Cabrera, 192
2. Mike Trout, 176
3. Chris Davis, 167
4. Jayson Werth, 160
5. Joey Votto, 156
   Paul Goldschmidt, 156

Votto wasn't cranking out RBIs, but his overall production was nothing short of elite.

So wRC+ and OPS+ can help you better understand individual output. And they can also help you compare players from entirely different eras and environments.

In 1968, Jim Wynn put up an .850 OPS for the Houston Astros. In 2000, Eric Chavez put up an .850 OPS for the Oakland A's.

Identical numbers, right?

Well, not so fast. The 1968 season was the so-called "Year of the Pitcher," when the league-wide OPS mark was .639—one of the lowest on record. And the 2000 season was the height of the game's offensive explosion, when the league-wide OPS was .782—one of the highest on record.

When taken in relation to the run-scoring environments in which they resided, the respective performances of Wynn and Chavez look a lot different. Wynn had a 159 wRC+ and a 158 OPS+, whereas Chavez had a 112 wRC+ and 117 OPS+. Both were above average, but Wynn was excellent in a season in which very few hitters knew the feeling.

These stats can also be illuminating when comparing players within a single season.

In 2018, for example, you would be hard-pressed to decide which American League third baseman had the more dynamic offensive season: José Ramírez of the Cleveland Indians or Alex Bregman of the Houston Astros. Ramírez had the higher OPS (.939 to Bregman's .926) and, perhaps as a result, won the Silver Slugger Award that year. But Bregman had the higher mark in both wRC+ (157 to Ramírez's 146) and OPS+ (156 to Ramírez's 150). This was a case in which digging into these context-driven numbers was important, because, while Houston's Minute Maid Park has generally been considered a hitter-friendly establishment, it actually played as a pitcher's park in 2018 (i.e., Astros hitters fared better on the road than at home, and Astros pitchers vice versa). Cleveland's Progressive Field, which is generally considered fair for both sides, played more into hitter's strengths that season. This helps explain why the "plus" numbers were more favorable for Bregman than Ramírez.

The scales for wRC+ and OPS+ are similar, and there are many instances in which the difference between the two can be miniscule or nonexistent. But the wRC+ calculation does tell us a bit more about a batter in that it operates as an extension of the wOBA formula, whereas OPS+ is an extension of the OPS formula. As previously discussed, wOBA does a better job than OPS at assigning proper weight to each event, in terms of its impact on run production, and so it is a better starting point.

But either metric will do a far better job of explaining a hitter's season or career in relation to those around him than OPS, batting average, ISO, Runs Created, or any other number we've covered in this book.

Sure, it would admittedly be preferable if both of these stats had catchier and less-clunky names (I don't know if wRC+ is supposed to be spoken out loud as "work-plus," but that's as relatable a translation as we're going to come up with). Still, until the next great stat comes along (and rest assured, it will), these are as good as it gets, and hopefully you've found the scale relatively easy to embrace.

Plus Stuff

Remember way back in the discussion about batting average, when we mentioned Khris Davis and his amazing maintenance of a .247 average in four consecutive seasons? Now that we've learned so much more about offensive metrics, we can take a more informed look at his track record.

Though Davis's batting average remained static from 2015 to 2018, his OPS marks, in succession, were .828, .831, .864, and .874. His OPS+ marks, in succession, were 123, 123, 131, and 136. And his wRC+ marks, in succession, were 122, 122, 129, and 135. So the 2015 and 2016 seasons were remarkably similar. All four seasons were well north of league average and, therefore, better than a .247 batting average would lead you to believe.

BsR (BASERUNNING)

What it is: *A baserunning statistic that takes stolen bases, caught stealing, and other baserunning plays (such as taking the extra base or being thrown out on the bases) into account and turns them into a value above or below the league average.*

What it is not: *The Baltic Sea Region.*

How it is calculated: *BsR = Weighted Stolen Base Runs + Ultimate Baserunning + Weighted Grounded Into Double Play Runs*

> *Weighted Stolen Base Runs (wSB) uses the league stolen-base data to estimate the number of runs above or below average a player contributes to his team by stealing bases or getting caught stealing.*
>
> *Ultimate Baserunning (UBR) gives a runner credit for advancement on the bases relative to the frequency with which the league average runner advances in the same situation.*
>
> *Weighted Grounded Into Double Play Runs (wGDB) calculates the extra outs a player saves or costs his team by hitting into fewer or more double plays than the average player with the same number of opportunities.*

Example: *Jimmy Rollins, SS, 2007 Philadelphia Phillies*

wSB	*UBR*	*wGDB*
5.0	*6.9*	*-0.1*

5.0 + 6.9 + (-0.1)

Jimmy Rollins's 2007 BsR was 11.8.

Why it matters: *Because with stolen-base attempts on a continual decline—and the art of baserunning extending beyond stolen bases—it's better to look at a context-driven and all-encompassing stat.*

Where you can find it: *FanGraphs.*

Back in the day, measuring speed in baseball wasn't precise.

Perhaps you've seen the video from that stunt in the summer of 1940, when the legendary Bob Feller stood on a closed-off street in Chicago and went into his windup as a police officer on a Harley revved up and roared by at 86 mph a few feet to his right. Seconds after the motorcycle passed, Feller flung his fastball to a paper target, with the ball catching and passing the motorcycle in midair and striking the bull's eye a split-second before the cop came crashing through. MLB deduced that Feller's fastball had traveled at a speed of 104 miles per hour.

Science!

For a while, that's how they measured pitch velocity in games, but too many motorcyclists were wiping out at the backstop.[13] Fortunately, velocity readings got quite a bit more reliable when radar guns arrived, and the Doppler readings that power MLB's sophisticated Statcast system (which we'll cover a bit more

---

13 Not really; just making sure you're paying attention.

in-depth within the final section of this book) give us greater accuracy than ever.

As for player speed, we've been even less speedy to evolve in our evaluations. Generally, the stat people rely on most to discern how fleet of foot a player is and how much value he's provided on the basepaths is the stolen base, which has been counted as a statistic since 1886. And so long as we view stolen-base counts with the understanding that the *caught stealing* count is equally informative (if you swipe 30 bags but also get caught 20 times, how much are you really helping your club?), there's nothing inherently wrong with using the stolen base as an—*ahem*—running tally.

But there's a big issue with steals in the modern game: teams are barely trying to compile them! The lightbulb has basically gone out on the green light. It's mostly stop signs and cautionary tales these days.

To illustrate the point, check out the number of league-wide stolen-base attempts per game over the last six decades:

1960s: 1.34
1970s: 1.93
1980s: 2.27
1990s: 2.13
2000s: 1.63
2010s: 1.55

As you can see, the game built toward a big steals spike in the '80s, when Rickey Henderson, Vince Coleman, and others were running wild, and has drifted back downward. The reason for that—like pretty much every change in the game over the last two decades—is analytically oriented. Number crunchers calculated the importance of delivering a pitch to the plate in less than 1.4 seconds to reduce steals, the necessity of succeeding at least three-quarters of the time if an attempted steal is even to be deemed worthwhile and, above all else, the value of an out in a game in which you only get 27 of them.

So they just don't run as much as they used to. In 1982, Henderson had more steals before the end of May (49) than 2019 stolen-base champ Mallex Smith had all season (46).

This leaves us in need of a better baserunning barometer.

Here, too, Statcast is helpful by offering up its Sprint Speed metric. It is just as it sounds: a measure of how many feet per second a player covers in his fastest one-second window. It has allowed us to gawk at the superhuman speed of guys like Billy Hamilton and Byron Buxton, and recent updates to include home-to-first times give us additional quickness context.

Sprint Speed is bound to influence any other baserunning metrics that are born in the coming years, but for now the stat that gives all others a run for their money (pun intended) in this category is BsR. It is the baserunning component of FanGraphs' version of Wins Above Replacement (WAR), which we'll discuss in the final section.

As you can see in the supplied formula, BsR is a simple calculation made up of complicated calculations. If you're super curious about the calculations that go into all those inputs, you can dig deeper on the FanGraphs site. But for our purposes here, what matters is that everything gets boiled down to a single metric, with the league average set to 0 instead of 100.[14]

You can run with this FanGraphs-crafted rule of thumb:

---

14 Note that caught stealing data prior to the 1950s is murky and the UBR calculation only dates back to 2002. These are factors to keep in mind when studying historical BsR marks.

Rating	BsR
Excellent	8
Great	6
Above Average	2
Average	0
Below Average	-2
Poor	-4
Awful	-6

The point of BsR is that there are ways for runners to add value which have nothing to do with stolen bases. Certainly, if you swipe a bag you are increasing your team's odds of producing a run. But you can also achieve value by taking the extra bag on a ball in play, tagging up on a fly ball, etc.

Consider this: In that aforementioned 1982 season, Henderson stole 130 bases total for the Oakland A's. That's a lot! As a matter of fact, that's the most ever in a modern-era season by a large margin (Lou Brock is second with 118 in 1974 with the St. Louis Cardinals).

Meanwhile, in '82, the NL league leader was Tim Raines of the Montreal Expos, who had 78 steals—or just 60 percent as many steals as Henderson. But when you look at BsR, the two were rated almost identically—Henderson at 9.5 and Raines at 9.3. UBR was not yet tracked in 1982, so the BsR scores from that season are mostly driven by a player's base-stealing efficiency. Yes, Henderson stole a ton of bases, but he was also caught 42 times (a 75.6 percent success ratio). Raines was caught just 16 times (an 83 percent success ratio). That's how he was able to close the BsR gap despite Henderson's stunning steals sum.

Born to (Base)Run

In the period which UBR data is available (dating back to 2002), the three highest single-season BsR marks belong to . . .

1. 14.3: Mike Trout, 2012 Los Angeles Angels
2. 14.1: Willy Taveras, 2008 Colorado Rockies
3. 14.0: Carlos Beltrán, 2003 Kansas City Royals

Taveras, who stole 68 bases in 2008, was a player with a well-below-average bat whose entire value rested in his legs and glove. But when you see that Trout (167 wRC+) and Beltrán (134 wRC+) had so much additive value on the bases—in addition to their prolific offensive numbers—it makes you appreciate them all the more.

SECTION 3
Pitching in and Catching on—The Best Pitching and Defense Stats

You might have looked at some of the mathematical mumbo jumbo that made up the calculations in the offensive chapters and considered them complicated. But if we take a step back and look at the big picture, a hitter's contributions to the game are way easier to calculate than a pitcher's contributions.

Why? Well, it's actually quite simple. The hitter is alone in the box. He acts independently. Whatever happens when bat meets (or does not meet) ball is attributable to him and him alone.

It doesn't work that way for pitchers. A pitcher and his defense are intertwined in the outcomes on the field, and so it is with this section of our crash course on analytics. It's only natural to pair pitching and defense, because defensive factors totally out of the pitcher's control can contribute to the runs he does or does not allow. If his fielders all have the range of a dead moth, guess what? He's going to give up a lot more runs than if he has a squad of Gold Glovers behind him.

So, in this section, we'll deliver the defensive data you can use in place of error counts to understand which players are good fielders, and we'll get into the pitching data you can use as an addendum to ERA to better understand a pitcher's prowess. We'll even look at the efforts that have been made to appraise pitching totally independent of defense.

ERA+ (ADJUSTED EARNED RUN AVERAGE)

What it is: *A pitcher's ERA, normalized across the entire league to account for external factors such as ballparks and opponents.*

What it is not: *Era Plus, a version of Era brand laundry detergent from the early 1990s that had extra stain-fighting power built in.*

How it is calculated: *ERA+ = League (AL/NL) ERA, adjusted for park factors x 100 / ERA*

> **Note:** We'll get into park factors in a later chapter, but the gist is that this calculation considers the run-scoring environment of the home ballpark the pitcher has pitched in (where 1.00 is neutral and anything above 1.00 is favorable to hitters and anything below 1.00 is favorable to pitchers).

Example: *Greg Maddux, RHP, 1995 Atlanta Braves*

ERA	1995 NL ERA	1995 Braves Park Factor
1.63	4.18	1.015

(4.18 x 1.015) x 100 / 1.63
(4.24 x 100) / 1.63

424 / 1.63

Greg Maddux's 1995 ERA+ was 260.

Why it matters: *Because while ERA does have some value in relaying how many earned runs a pitcher allows per nine innings, the lack of provided context regarding the run-scoring environment in a given year—or in a pitcher's home park—makes using ERA to compare pitchers a dicey proposition.*

Where you can find it: *Baseball Reference. And as we'll note below, FanGraphs has a variation called ERA-.*

In early 2018, when Mike Mussina became a Hall of Famer, the question immediately arose: "Mike Mussina is a Hall of Famer?!"

I heard it from friends. I heard it from readers. Heck, I even heard it from the editor of this very book. In the midst of some email banter about this project, here's what Jason Katzman wrote to me:

"Do you really think that Mussina is a HOFer? He only had one full season where his ERA was under three (2.54 in 1992) and six seasons where it was over four (and was 5.15 in 2007). I understand that he won 270 games. However, while Roy Halladay pitched two fewer seasons, he had three 20-win seasons, six seasons with an ERA under three, and two Cy Young Awards. I just don't see how you can say that both are worthy when comparing those numbers. If you disagree, I'd love to hear your thoughts."

Well, Jason, I do disagree (but you knew this already from my email reply), and there is no better place to share my thoughts than here in the ERA+ discussion. For this is a stat that helps us better understand the Mike Mussinas of the world, who simply pitched in the wrong places at the wrong times to be fully appreciated.

Mussina reached the big leagues in 1991 and walked away in 2008 (ironically, after his only 20-win season). To Jason's point, he rarely overwhelmed in the ERA department in that long span. His lone sub-3.00 ERA season was his first full season. He pitched his entire career in the AL and never once led it in ERA. He never finished higher than fourth in the Cy Young voting (though, to his credit, he did finish in the top six of voting nine times). If that's all you knew about Mussina, you'd probably relegate him to the bin of "good, but not great." In fact, here are some pitchers who have lower career ERAs than Mussina's 3.68 mark and comparable career innings to his 3,562 2/3 that are *not* in the Hall of Fame:

- Joe Niekro: 3.59 ERA, 3,584 1/3 innings
- Bob Friend: 3.58 ERA, 3,611 innings
- Mickey Lolich: 3.44 ERA, 3,638 1/3 innings
- Paul Derringer: 3.46 ERA, 3,645 innings
- Jerry Reuss: 3.64 ERA, 3,669 2/3 innings
- Jerry Koosman: 3.36 ERA, 3,839 1/3 innings

If Moose is in, shouldn't all these guys be in?

In a word, no.

When we look at those ERA marks, we aren't taking important environmental factors into account. Consider Niekro. He's in the National Polish-American Sports Hall of Fame (*Gratulacje*, Joe!), but not the National Baseball Hall of Fame. The knuckleballer's career covered the 1967 to 1988 seasons, a span in which teams scored an average of 4.18 runs per game. His best stretch was probably the 10 1/2 seasons he spent with Houston, where he pitched his home games in the Astrodome, a cavernous and notoriously pitcher-friendly building.

Mussina, on the other hand, pitched in a period when an average of 4.77 runs per team per game were scored. And he pitched the entirety of his home games in Camden Yards and Yankee Stadium—parks that, as a result of their short porches and inviting power alleys, routinely rate as hitter-friendly. He spent his entire career in the loaded AL East, in the midst of the so-called steroid era.

We need some way to statistically account for these differences, and this is where ERA+ swoops in for the rescue (and, as a result, swoops Mussina into Cooperstown).

Like OPS+ and wRC+, ERA+ scales league average to 100. So, again, 110 is 10 percent better than average and 90 is 10 percent worse than average. Here's a rating scale to work with:

Rating	ERA+
Excellent	160
Great	130
Above Average	120
Average	100
Below Average	90
Poor	80
Awful	70

Again, Mussina's 3.68 career ERA puts him behind Niekro and 140 other pitchers with at least 2,500 career innings in the modern era. That's not Hall of Fame stuff. But Mussina's 123 ERA+ puts him above all but 32 pitchers with that innings minimum (including Niekro, who has a 98 ERA+).

Now that's more like it.

Mussina might have run into some difficulty when it came to opponents in his prime, but he was fortunate that his Hall of Fame eligibility overlapped with an increased awareness among members of the BBWAA of how a stat such as ERA+ can put a career in proper perspective. It is true that Mussina never had a league-leading ERA, but he did have 11 full seasons in which his ERA+ was anywhere from 25 to 64 percent better than the league average. He was one of the best pitchers of an era in which offense had (because of bigger bodies and smaller parks) exploded.

So, as you can now see, ERA+ can shine a light on underrated arms, and it can also help us properly glorify the greats. To stick with Mussina's era, we're all familiar with the work of Pedro Martínez, right? We agree that he was deserving of his first-ballot Hall of Fame election, yes? But do you realize Pedro might have had—gulp—*the greatest starting pitching season of all time?*

Look, I'm not saying it's definitely true; I'm just saying it's not definitely *not* true. See for yourself:

- Pedro Martínez, 2000 Boston Red Sox:
  291 ERA+, 217 innings
- Walter Johnson, 1913 Washington Senators:
  259 ERA+, 346 innings
- Bob Gibson, 1968 St. Louis Cardinals:
  258 ERA+, 304 2/3 innings
- Pedro Martínez, 1999 Boston Red Sox:
  243 ERA+, 213 1/3 innings
- Walter Johnson, 1912 Washington Senators:
  243 ERA+, 369 innings

OK, so he might not have thrown well north of 300 innings like "The Big Train" did (and in a related story, he is still in possession of his right arm), but those two seasons in the thick of the steroid era are about as impressive a display of pitching dominance as we'll ever see. Gibson's '68 special rivals that of Elvis Presley and, because it featured the lowest ERA (1.12) of the live ball era, is often pointed to as the gold standard. But ERA+ takes just a little bit of the shine off that season because run production was disastrously low league-wide in the "Year of the Pitcher," to the point that they lowered the mound the following season.

Look at it this way: Gibson had a 1.12 ERA in a season in which the average major-league ERA was 2.98.

Pedro had a 1.74 ERA in a season (2000) in which the major-league ERA was . . . 4.76!

For what it's worth, Martínez is also the all-time record-holder for career ERA+ among those with 2,500 innings, with a 154 mark. So you can make a statistical argument that he's the greatest starting pitcher of all time, if you're so inclined.[1]

Now, I know some of you are still aghast at the argument that Bob Gibson did not have the greatest pitching season of all time, and I totally get and respect that. But I have another complicated concept to introduce here, and that's a little thing called ERA-, which is available at FanGraphs.

I know, I know. This sounds like some twisted joke. We've just grown accustomed to the plus concept, and now I'm trying to sneak a minus past you. And the weird thing here is that the minus and the plus are basically two variations of the same thing. What the FanGraphs model does is invert the fraction used to calculate ERA+. So ERA over league ERA, as opposed to league ERA over ERA. This means that, with ERA-, the further *below* 100 (which still represents league average) you are, the better.

Logically, this makes sense. The goal of pitching, after all, is to keep scores down, not raise them up. So if you prefer a stat that reflects this idea, by all means, venture over to FanGraphs and use ERA-. But I chose to highlight ERA+ in this chapter for two reasons:

1. It more closely resembles the offensive concepts of wRC+ and OPS+ that we covered earlier.
2. To my eye, it is far more commonly cited in media coverage of baseball than ERA- is.[2]

---

1 Because of the vast innings discrepancy between Pedro and his contemporary Roger Clemens and the likes of Walter Johnson, Christy Mathewson, Cy Young, etc., I'm not quite willing to go there.

2 Beyond those reasonable reasons are a couple other, goofier ones. From a purely psychological perspective, pluses are more pleasing than minuses. And from a purely aesthetic point of view, I personally like the wider range of numbers associated with ERA+. Pedro's 2000 season, for instance, rates as a 35 ERA-, which is great but somehow doesn't set off the same alarm bells as that 291 ERA+ does.

Whether you choose to use the plus or the minus, the bottom line to all of this is that plain old ERA—our go-to pitching metric for many, many years—has let us down by not telling us enough.

But thankfully, it didn't keep Mussina out of the Hall of Fame.[3]

Did You Mo?

If we invite relievers into the ERA+ conversation by lowering the career minimum to 1,000 innings, then longtime Yankees closer Mariano Rivera, who joined his old teammate Mussina on the Cooperstown induction dais via the first-ever unanimous selection in 2018, is your ERA+ standard-bearer with an incredible 205 mark. It just goes to show that if you are 105 percent better than league average, you will appear on 100 percent of Hall of Fame ballots.

---

3   Editor's note: Point made.

WHIP (WALKS PLUS HITS PER INNING PITCHED)

What it is: *A means of evaluating how well a pitcher has kept runners off the basepaths.*

What it is not: *A strip of leather used for flogging a person or urging an animal along, or a Congress member tasked with ensuring attendance or voting in debates.*

How it is calculated: *WHIP = Walks + Hits / Innings Pitched*

Example: *Tom Seaver, RHP, 1971 New York Mets*

Walks	*Hits*	*Innings Pitched*
61	*210*	*286 1/3*

61 + 210 / 286.3333
271 / 286.3333

Tom Seaver's 1971 WHIP was 0.946.

Why it matters: *Because, as is the case on your morning commute, traffic is bad. WHIP tells us how well a pitcher has performed the very fundamental role of not letting the traffic pile up—obviously an important element in run prevention.*

Where you can find it: *MLB.com, Baseball Reference, FanGraphs, ESPN.com, etc.*

What's the one thing pitchers hate more than the DH rule? Baserunners, of course! So they love to crack that WHIP.

Unlike some other numbers covered in this book, the formula for WHIP is blissfully simple. With that simplicity comes the caveat that WHIP shouldn't be taken as a definitive evaluation point. But much like farmers use a whip to herd their cattle, we can use WHIP to guide our brains toward proper analysis of a pitcher's performance.

Really, WHIP is somewhat akin to OBP in that the quick and dirty math leads to some intellectual discrepancies, but the ease of understanding what is good and what is bad helps make it more mainstream than other, more highfalutin figures.

Though the league average WHIP fluctuates from year to year, here's how FanGraphs dishes out the WHIP cream:

Rating	WHIP
Excellent	1.00 and under
Great	1.10
Above Average	1.20
Average	1.30
Below Average	1.40
Poor	1.50
Awful	1.60 and higher

Writer and editor Daniel Okrent introduced this stat in 1980—initially calling it "IPRAT," for "innings pitched ratio"—in conjunction with his creation of Rotisserie baseball. Because this was in those prehistoric days where every bit of baseball minutiae (and other life minutiae) was not available at the click of a mouse, he had to rely on the Sunday newspaper for his stats. And because the Sunday newspaper did not include hit batsmen in their weekly statistical updates, hit batsmen were not—and still are not—included in the WHIP calculation.[4]

"I'd always felt that the number of base runners was the single greatest determinant of pitcher performance," Okrent told the *New York Times* in 2013. "It turned out it did correlate."

Among retired pitchers, the top modern-era career WHIP marks belong to Hall of Famers Addie Joss (0.968), Ed Walsh (1.000), Mariano Rivera (1.000), Pedro Martínez (1.054), Christy Mathewson (1.058), Trevor Hoffman (1.058), Walter Johnson (1.061), and Mordecai Brown (1.066). So you can see what Okrent's talking about.

Where WHIP whiffs is in its inability to differentiate between types of hits. As in batting average, extra bases don't carry extra weight in WHIP. And, obviously, home runs are more in the control of the pitcher than other types of hits, in which the pitcher is often at the mercy of his defense and, as we discussed in Section 1, error judgments aren't always applied accurately. It is preferable to look at a pitcher's opponents' OBP for a more mathematically consistent view of the traffic he allowed.

Then again, because it is based on individual events and not sequences, a pitcher's WHIP is not as susceptible to major fluctuations due to one misplay the way ERA is. So, again, it's a fine starting point.

WHIP can be especially helpful in evaluating relievers, for whom ERA marks can be especially erratic, given the smaller innings sample size.

"You have one bad outing, and it kind of messes your ERA up," Toronto Blue Jays reliever Ryan Tepera told MLB.com in 2018. "And sometimes, you might leave one runner out there and you don't even give up that run. You're not given a chance to get

---

4 Neither, you'll note, are errors and batters who reach via fielder's choice, but obviously those are left out for good reason.

out of the inning. Somebody else gives it up. I think WHIP is a little bit more of a personal thing and a better gauge of how your year went."

The next time you look up a pitcher's ERA, follow that up by looking at his WHIP, because the latter can be a decent indicator as to whether the former is firm or flimsy. A pitcher with a low ERA and a high WHIP isn't likely to maintain that discrepancy for long. In 2010, for example, St. Louis Cardinals left-hander Jaime García managed to post an ERA of 2.70 in 163 1/3 innings despite a WHIP of 1.316. The next three seasons all yielded similar WHIP marks—1.320, 1.364, and 1.301—but his ERA in that three-year span was almost exactly one full point higher, at 3.68.

You can call that WHIPlash.

WHIP it Good

Nobody WHIPped their opponents quite like Boston Red Sox reliever Koji Uehara in 2013. His 0.565 WHIP didn't just break—it blew away—the record of 0.607 that had been set by Dennis Eckersley in 1989 for pitchers with at least 50 innings in a season. Uehara's opponents had a laughable .130/.163/.237 slash line against him, and he was the first pitcher in history to walk fewer than 10 batters while striking out 100.

GSc (GAME SCORE)

What it is: *A measure of a starting pitcher's performance in a specific game.*

What it is not: *Your point total when you play Pac-Man at the arcade.*

How it is calculated: *Start with 50 points. Add one point for each out recorded (in other words, three points for every complete inning pitched). Add two points for each inning completed after the fourth. Add one point for each strikeout. Subtract two points for each hit allowed. Subtract four points for each earned run allowed. Subtract two points for each unearned run allowed. Subtract one point for each walk.*

Example: *Bob Gibson's Game Seven start vs. the Boston Red Sox in the 1967 World Series*

Innings Pitched	Strikeouts	Hits
9 (27 outs)	10	3

Earned Runs	Unearned Runs	Walks
2	0	3

50 + (1 x 27) + (2 x 5) + (1 x 10) - (2 x 3) - (4 x 2) - (2 x 0) - (1 x 3)
50 + 27 + 10 + 10 - 6 - 8 - 0 - 3

Bob Gibson's 1967 Game Seven Game Score was 80.

Why it matters: *Because the official statistic Quality Start does not distinguish the degree of caliber between one Quality Start and* *another. This stat basically boils a starting pitching line down to its essence and eases the process of comparing starts.*

Where you can find it: *Baseball Reference, within each pitcher's game logs.*

Some of the numbers available to the astute baseball analyst are staggering in their complexity, diabolical in their design, and elemental in their importance. They deservedly have a place not just in basic baseball banter, but in eminent applications such as award and Hall of Fame voting.

Game Score is not one of those numbers . . . but rather just meant to be fun.

Bill James came up with Game Score and, judging by what he said when he unleashed it upon the world in the 1980s, it's not his favorite creation. In *The Bill James Historical Abstract's* paperback update in 1988, James wrote of Game Score: "[It's] a kind of garbage stat that I present not because it helps us understand anything in particular but because it is fun to play around with."

Hey, you know what they say. One man's trash . . .

Whether GSc is detritus data is debatable, but James was right that it is fun to play around with. I might have joked above that it's not the same as a Pac-Man point total, but it has the same effect of providing the allure of accumulation. Granted, we don't typically tabulate GSc as the game itself is unfolding (we tend to be more preoccupied by the *actual* score). But now that you know the calculation, maybe give it a try the next time a pitchers' duel breaks out at a ballpark near you.

Game Score began as a means of contextualizing Roger Clemens's 20-strikeout, three-hit, one-run performance for the Boston Red Sox vs. the Seattle Mariners in 1986. Clemens was the first pitcher to amass 20 Ks in a nine-inning game, and the mark has only been reached three times since (once by Clemens himself, a decade later).

So that's a great place to start using Game Score—as a means of sorting out the 20-K starts.

20-Strikeout Game	Game Score
Kerry Wood, CHC, May 6, 1998 vs. HOU	105
Roger Clemens, BOS, Sept. 18, 1996 vs. DET	97
Roger Clemens, BOS, April 29, 1986 vs. SEA	97
Max Scherzer, WSH, May 11, 2016 vs. DET	87

As you can see, not all 20-strikeout gems are created equal (well, unless you're Clemens, apparently). Scherzer gave up two home runs in his game, so that easily docked him a few points. Clemens gave up a run on three hits in the game against the Mariners in '86 and allowed five hits in his nine scoreless innings against the Tigers in '96.

Wood, meanwhile, pitched nine scoreless with just one hit allowed. So not only does his masterful afternoon against the Astros rank first on this particular list, it's the highest Game Score of all time.

That's right. It ranks ahead of the 23 so-called "perfect" games in MLB history. Wood might have given up a hit (darn you and your infield single, Ricky Gutiérrez!), but he was somehow better than "perfect."[5]

Of course, Wood wasn't perfect on the GSc scale. To achieve that version of perfection (a score of 114), all a pitcher has to do is toss a perfect game in which every out is a strikeout.

---

5   For what it's worth, the two highest Game Scores in a perfect game belong to the Dodgers' Sandy Koufax (101, on September 9, 1965 vs. Cubs) and to the Giants' Matt Cain (101, on June 13, 2012 vs. Astros), both of whom logged 14 strikeouts in their perfectos.

Piece of cake, right?

Because the perfect score of 114 isn't likely to happen anytime soon, here's a realistic way of evaluating a pitching performance based on GSc, courtesy of FanGraphs:

Rating	Game Score
Make Sure Your Friends Are Watching	90–100
Excellent	80–90
Great	70–80
Good	60–70
Above Average	50–60
Below Average	40–50
Poor	30–40
Bad	20–30
Awful	10–20
Unspeakable	0–10

The vast majority of seasons produce at least 10 performances that rate as a 90 or higher. The 2015 season had 31 of them—the most in a single season since the advent of the designated hitter rule in 1973. But as pitching roles continue to (d)evolve and starters don't go as deep into games, the 90+ score could become something of an endangered species.

Of course, because those games in which the starter simply doesn't have it will always crop up, poor scores are a part of the picture. Back in 2006, there were a record 13 instances in which pitchers posted a GSc of zero or below. St. Louis Cardinals right-hander Jason Marquis had two starts that season in which he gave up double-digit run and hit totals in only five innings of work, so he has the rare distinction of two sub-zero Game Scores (more like Game Sores) in a single season. There have been 30 major-league seasons in which the entire league didn't register more than one such outing.

The lowest GSc on record for a nine-inning game belongs to Hod Lisenbee. On September 11, 1936, Lisenbee, pitching for the Philadelphia A's, allowed 17 runs (14 earned) on a record-tying 26 hits with four walks and only one strikeout against the Chicago White Sox. That's a calamitous -35 on the GSc scale. But in Lisenbee's defense, he was thrown to the wolves that day. A's manager Connie Mack had opted to minimize the number of pitchers he brought on a road trip, and it was up to the 37-year-old Lisenbee to go the distance no matter what. And the "what," in this instance, was ugly.

So how seriously should we take Game Score? James didn't intend for it to be more than a diversion, and the formula has some flaws. Hit batsmen, such as the one Wood plunked in his famous game, don't count, and there is no differentiation between intentional walks issued by a manager and walks that are more attributable to pitching performance. Furthermore, there is no differentiation between types of hits. And comparing Game Scores—much like ERAs—across eras can be misleading, depending on the offensive environment a pitcher is working in.

But GSc can be used in aggregate to give a snapshot of a season, or even a career. In the live ball era (beginning in 1920), Sandy Koufax's 1963 season featured the most "great" (GSc of 70 or above) starts, with 28. Koufax won the Cy Young and the NL MVP that year. According to the research from Scott Lindholm of the analysis website BeyondtheBoxScore.com, Nolan Ryan has the highest cumulative GSc (46,262) in history, which speaks to his incredible longevity. Pedro Martínez (61.2), Bob Gibson (61.0), and Tom Seaver (60.3) have the three highest career Game Score averages among those with at least 400 starts, which speaks to their day-to-day dominance.

Most importantly, GSc does a much better job contextualizing a performance than the oft-cited Quality Start stat.

A Quality Start—a stat invented by sportswriter John Lowe in 1985—is one in which the pitcher goes at least six innings and gives up three earned runs or fewer. If you happened to have a 30-start season in which you went exactly six innings and gave up exactly three earned runs every time, you would have 30 Quality Starts, sure. But you'd also have an unflattering 4.50 ERA.

With that in mind, compare these two hypothetical performances:

- Pitcher A: 6 innings pitched, 4 runs allowed (3 earned), 6 hits, 4 walks, 5 strikeouts
- Pitcher B: 9 innings pitched, 4 runs allowed (all earned), 7 hits, 1 walk, 9 strikeouts

Pitcher A is credited with a Quality Start, but his Game Score is only 47, or "below average." Pitcher B doesn't get a QS, but his GSc is 65, or "good."

Which stat would you say did a better job of relaying the overall quality of the pitcher's performance? If you answered Game Score, you've obviously been keeping score.

Know the Score

Entering 2020, there had only been 16 performances in history with a GSc of 100 or higher in a nine-inning game, according to Baseball Reference. Scherzer didn't achieve this feat with his 20-strikeout game, but he does appear on this list twice:

GSc	Player	Date	Tm	Opp	Rslt	IP	H	R	ER	BB	SO
105	Kerry Wood	5/6/1998	CHC	HOU	W 2–0	9	1	0	0	0	20
104	Max Scherzer	10/3/2015 (2)	WSN	NYM	W 2–0	9	0	0	0	0	17
102	Clayton Kershaw	6/18/2014	LAD	COL	W 8–0	9	0	0	0	0	15
101	Nap Rucker	9/5/1908 (2)	BRO	BSN	W 6–0	9	0	0	0	0	14
101	Sandy Koufax	9/9/1965	LAD	CHC	W 1–0	9	0	0	0	0	14
101	Nolan Ryan	5/1/1991	TEX	TOR	W 3–0	9	0	0	0	2	16
101	Matt Cain	6/13/2012	SFG	HOU	W 10–0	9	0	0	0	0	14
100	Warren Spahn	9/16/1960	MLN	PHI	W 4–0	9	0	0	0	2	15
100	Nolan Ryan	7/9/1972	CAL	BOS	W 3–0	9	1	0	0	1	16
100	Nolan Ryan	7/15/1973	CAL	DET	W 6–0	9	0	0	0	4	17
100	Curt Schilling	4/7/2002	ARI	MIL	W 2–0	9	1	0	0	2	17
100	Randy Johnson	5/18/2004	ARI	ATL	W 2–0	9	0	0	0	0	13
100	Brandon Morrow	8/8/2010	TOR	TBR	W 1–0	9	1	0	0	2	17
100	Max Scherzer	6/14/2015	WSN	MIL	W 4–0	9	1	0	0	1	16
100	Gerrit Cole	5/4/2018	HOU	ARI	W 8–0	9	1	0	0	1	16
100	Justin Verlander	9/1/2019	HOU	TOR	W 2–0	9	0	0	0	1	14

FIP (FIELDING INDEPENDENT PITCHING)

What it is: *A pitching measurement similar to ERA but focused solely on events a pitcher has the most control over—strikeouts, unintentional walks, hit by pitches, and home runs.*

What it is not: *Feline Infectious Peritonitis.*

How it is calculated: *FIP = ((Home Runs x 13) + (3 x (Walks + Hit By Pitches)) - (2 x Strikeouts)) / Innings Pitched + FIP Constant*

> **Note:** The FIP Constant (contrary to what you might think with something called a "constant") can change from year to year, based on the league's run-scoring environment, but is usually around 3.10. It is used solely to bring FIP onto a relatable ERA scale. The FIP constant for each season can be found at FanGraphs.

Example: *Clayton Kershaw, LHP, 2015 Los Angeles Dodgers*

Home Runs	Walks	Hit By Pitch	Strikeouts
15	42	5	301

Innings Pitched	2015 FIP Constant
232 2/3	3.134

((15 x 13) + (3 x (42 + 5)) - (2 x 301) / 232.6667 + 3.134
195 + 141 - 602 / 232.6667 + 3.134

-266 / 232.6667 + 3.134

-1.14 + 3.134

Clayton Kershaw's 2015 FIP was 1.99.

Why it matters: *Because by limiting the inputs strictly to the events a pitcher has the most control over, FIP is a better tool than ERA— which is influenced by the whims of a pitcher's defense or the rulings of an official scorer—in evaluating a pitcher's effectiveness. A pitcher has little control over what happens once the ball is put in play.*

Where you can find it: *Baseball Reference and FanGraphs.*

You're driving a car down a two-lane road. You're obeying the speed limit. Your seat belt is buckled. Your hands are at ten and two. You're not texting or tweeting or emailing or reading this eBook.

You are, in other words, in control and adept and alert and doing everything a responsible driver should do.

Just then, suddenly and without warning, the driver in front of you slams on his brakes. You swerve to avoid hitting his car and run yourself off the road and into a tree.

Who was at fault here? You, the responsible, law-abiding, upstanding citizen with the unimpeachable driving performance and now-totaled car? Or the other guy who sped away with no concern for the wreck he just left behind?

In legal mumbo jumbo, they call this unfortunate situation in which a person suffers a difficult fate through no fault of their own a "no-contact car accident" caused by a "phantom driver."

In baseball, for the longest time, they just called it bad luck.

Pitchers can basically control only one thing: the pitch they throw. Anything that happens after that, short of a comebacker or a play to the right-hand side of the infield that forces them to cover first base, is out of their control. And yet the individual metric most commonly used to assess a pitcher—ERA—can sometimes become inflated by outcomes that have absolutely nothing to do with the pitch that was thrown, even though it only focuses on "earned" runs.

That, in a nutshell, is why we have Fielding Independent Pitching, or FIP.

If you're not hip to FIP, this history trip will help you get a grip.

Before there was FIP, there were DIPS—or Defense Independent Pitching Stats. DIPS changed baseball forever. It upended the way people—major-league executives included—looked at pitchers, because it successfully challenged the notion that pitchers have influence on the number of hits resulting from balls put in play.

The concept of DIPS was first put forward by a paralegal and part-time Rotisserie leaguer named Voros McCracken. If that name sounds made up, it's because it is (unfortunately). His real name is Robert McCracken, and Voros is a nickname derived from his Hungarian heritage. So not only was this man smart enough to realize elements like defense, ballpark, weather, and sheer randomness could greatly affect a pitcher's ERA, he was also smart enough to recognize that Voros McCracken is a heck of a lot more memorable a name than Robert McCracken.

After posting his theories behind DIPS on an Internet message board in 1999, McCracken formally published them in an article on the *Baseball Prospectus* website in 2001.

"My belief?" McCracken wrote. "Well, simply that hits allowed are not a particularly meaningful statistic in the evaluation of pitchers."

Does that sound insane to you? Because it certainly sounded insane to people in 2001. But McCracken studied the data and found little correlation between how many hits per ball in play a given pitcher allows one year versus the next. Walks, strikeouts, and home runs generally correlated pretty well. So a pitcher with a high strikeout rate and a low walk rate one year could reasonably be counted on to have a high strikeout rate and low walk rate the next. But the rate of hits per balls in play fluctuated wildly.

McCracken pointed to a couple notable examples: In 1998, Greg Maddux's opponents hit .267 on balls put in the field of play (so not including homers), and that was the fourth lowest such mark posted by any qualified pitcher in baseball. But in 1999, that average ballooned to .324—the seventh highest in all of baseball. And then, in 2000, it dropped back down to .277, the twelfth lowest.

Pedro Martínez saw a similar pattern in those seasons: .272 in 1998 (tenth lowest in baseball), .325 in '99 (eighth highest), and .237 in '00 (absolute lowest). You can get seasick with sways like that.

So what happened? Did Maddux and Martínez suddenly forget how to pitch between 1998 and '99, and then suddenly remember again in 2000? Nope. External factors—especially defense—contributed to these large fluctuations from year to year.

McCracken's article sparked a wave of interest. Though baseball writer and historian Craig R. Wright correctly challenged McCracken's assertions in noting that certain types of pitchers—specifically knuckleballers and fly-ball pitchers—have greater influence on the outcome of balls in play than other types of pitchers, McCracken's general premise was deemed correct after further study from Bill James in his 2001 edition of *The Bill James Historical Abstract*.

"I feel stupid for not having realized it thirty years ago," James wrote.

There would be many other studies in the years that followed, and it would generally be agreed upon that pitchers *do* have some control over the type of contact allowed (ground ball or fly ball). But still, the basic point remained: We can learn more about a pitcher's performance from his strikeouts, walks, and homers allowed than from his hits allowed.

So that's how we got to FIP. It is one of several metrics that branched off of DIPS, including SIERA (Skill Interactive ERA), tERA (True Earned Run Average), LIPS (Luck Independent Pitching Statistics), and DRA (Deserved Run Average). All of these are members of the DIPS family tree, and McCracken deserves credit for planting the first seed.

But FIP, which was developed by Tom Tango (another made-up name by a gentleman who preferred to keep his real identity a secret), is by far the most widely cited of the defense-independent pitching numbers. So here we are.

If you eliminate the FIP constant from the equation, you get what can be called a "raw" FIP, where zero is pretty good and below zero is ideal. But in Tango's creation of FIP, it was wisely decided that bringing it to an ERA scale makes for an easier means of understanding how a pitcher's FIP relates to his ERA.

Because it is scaled to reflect ERA; the same numbers that make for a good ERA make for a good FIP. Here's the FanGraphs rule of thumb on FIP:

Rating	FIP
Excellent	3.20
Great	3.50
Above Average	3.80
Average	4.20
Below Average	4.40
Poor	4.70
Awful	5.00

A pitcher's FIP can oscillate quite a bit from outing to outing, so it's better to look at a full season's worth of FIP data than, say, a month's worth. But by subtracting FIP from ERA, you can get a sense of how factors out of the pitcher's control may have inflated his ERA.

Conversely, you might find examples of guys who have actually been saved by their defense from an ERA more unflattering than the one they are carrying.

One example from the latter category that stands out is former Toronto Blue Jays pitcher Ricky Romero. If you looked only at the traditional numbers going into 2012, Romero looked like a sneaky AL Cy Young candidate. His win total and innings pitched had increased each of the previous three seasons, and his ERA had dropped from 4.30 in 2009 to 3.73 in '10 to 2.92 in '11.

Ah, but the FIP Monster was looming beneath the surface. Though Romero's ERA had fallen 81 points between 2010 and '11, his FIP had climbed from 3.64 to 4.20. The 1.28-point difference between his 2011 ERA and FIP marks was one of the largest of any qualified pitcher in the 2010s.

So while Romero's steep fall from grace in 2012, when he went 9–14, walked 105 batters, and posted a 5.77 ERA was jarring, maybe we shouldn't have been totally shocked. By 2013, the answer to the question, "Wherefore art thou, Romero?" was Triple-A Buffalo. He never made it back to the big leagues before officially retiring in 2018.

On the flip side of the equation is what happened with veteran right-hander Edinson Vólquez. In 2013, the former All-Star looked washed up. The San Diego Padres released him in August with a 6.01 ERA in 27 starts. And though things worked out a little bit better with the Los Angeles Dodgers in the last month or so of that season (going 0–2 in 5 starts with a 4.18 ERA), he entered free agency with a 5.71 ERA overall between the two stops.

But Vólquez's FIP that season was 4.24, and the Pittsburgh Pirates, wisely surmising that their strong defensive cast could more ably support Vólquez, gave him a chance with a one-year, $5 million contract.

The Pirates went on to watch him post a resurgent 2014 season in which his 3.04 ERA made him the ace of their staff. (He fared far better in free agency the following winter, netting a two-year, $20 million deal with the Kansas City Royals.)

So FIP is best used in trying to determine if a pitcher is perhaps due for regression or improvement in his future ERA. And because it is tied to things the pitcher most strongly controls, it is a far better predictor of future performance than ERA itself.

Granted, the Romero and Vólquez examples are extreme ones. And FIP, like ERA itself, isn't foolproof.

But the idea of how something so elemental (hits and, ergo, runs allowed) in how we view pitching performance can be skewed so substantially by things that have nothing to do with pitching itself is strongly worth considering—and FIP puts a number to that idea.

By the way, if you like FIP, you'll love xFIP. Developed by Dave Studeman at HardballTimes.com (and viewable at FanGraphs), xFIP tries to account for the randomness of home run results.

If a pitcher has a major fluctuation in his home-run-per-fly-ball-rate, xFIP—a sort of FIP replacement, without the recovery time that comes with a hip replacement—adjusts accordingly based on the pitcher's typical fly-ball rate. Because reliable HR/FB ratios are only available going back to 2002, xFIP information is only available for less than two decades of play. Even so, it can be used as a quick forecast of what sort of ERA a pitcher can reasonably be counted on to post based on all the underlying data. Plus, as the game goes on, more data will be collected to provide more solid figures.

FIP-a-Dee-Doo-Dah

Only six pitchers in the live ball era have qualified for the ERA title while posting both an ERA and a FIP mark below 2.00. They are:

- Hal Newhouser, 1946 Detroit Tigers:
  1.88 ERA, 1.97 FIP
- Sandy Koufax, 1963 Los Angeles Dodgers:
  1.88 ERA, 1.85 FIP
- Bob Gibson, 1968 St. Louis Cardinals:
  1.12 ERA, 1.77 FIP
- Tom Seaver, 1971 New York Mets:
  1.76 ERA, 1.93 FIP[6]
- Clayton Kershaw, 2014 Los Angeles Dodgers:
  1.77 ERA, 1.81 FIP
- Jacob deGrom, 2018 New York Mets:
  1.70 ERA, 1.99 FIP

---

6 Seaver did not win the Cy Young Award that season, instead going to Fergie Jenkins of the Chicago Cubs, who had an ERA of 2.77 and a FIP of 2.38. Jenkins went 24–13 that season, while Seaver went 20–10, making the case that wins may have had a bearing on this decision.

MISCELLANEOUS PITCHING STATS

We've made our pitch for ERA+, WHIP, and FIP as worthwhile means of studying a pitcher's season. But here are some other stats that will arm you with quality data.

FB% (Fly-Ball Rate), LD% (Line-Drive Rate), GB% (Ground-Ball Rate), IFFB% (Infield Fly-Ball Rate)

Every ball put into play is characterized as a fly ball, line drive, ground ball or pop-up, so these stats tell you which percentage of batted balls against a particular pitcher fall into each of those four categories. These rates can also be used to evaluate hitters, but you will most frequently see them used in relation to pitchers.

Fly-ball and ground-ball rates are especially helpful in telling us what kind of pitcher we are looking at. Those with high fly-ball rates tend to allow more home runs, and those with high ground-ball rates tend to induce more double plays.

Per FanGraphs, which has batted-ball data going back to 2002, these are the league average rates for each of these stats:

Rate	League Average
FB	35%
LD	21%
GB	44%
IFFB	11%

K% (Strikeout Rate) and BB% (Walk Rate)

These are the percentages of plate appearances that end in these two particular outcomes. Again, they are available for both pitchers and hitters, but you'll more frequently see them cited in relation to pitchers.

Pitchers who are able to frequently induce weak contact don't need a high K rate to be successful, but it is not uncommon to see the K rate leaderboards dotted with the game's best pitchers.

A pitcher with a high walk rate can be successful if it's paired with a high strikeout rate. But given that one of a pitcher's primary goals is to avoid base traffic, a high walk rate is generally a red flag, as walks—unlike batted balls—are not a product of team defense or luck.

> **Note:** You'll often see strikeout and walk rates expressed as K/9 or BB/9 (strikeouts or walks per nine innings), but the flaw with these rates is that they only take outs into account for the denominator. So a pitcher might have a relatively high K/9 rate while also giving up a ton of hits and walks that aren't considered in the equation—unlike in K%, where all plate appearances are involved.

This book is being written at a time in which there is a high proliferation of strikeouts at the major-league level (and the rate is climbing annually), so the averages vary from year to year. But here's a rule of thumb from FanGraphs on how to evaluate these rates:

Rating	K%	BB%
Excellent	27.0	4.5
Great	24.0	5.5
Above Average	22.0	6.5
Average	20.0	7.7
Below Average	17.0	8.0
Poor	15.0	8.5
Awful	13.0	9.0

K/BB (Strikeout to Walk Ratio)

Quite simply, the number of strikeouts a pitcher records for each walk he allows. All you do is divide the strikeouts by the walks to come to this important pitching reference point, which is telling because it looks at two of the outcomes a pitcher has the most control over.

If you want to take K/BB a step further, you can check out K%-BB% at FanGraphs, and it is exactly as it looks: the pitcher's walk rate subtracted from his strikeout rate. But K/BB is the more commonly cited metric. Obviously, the higher the K/BB, the better. Here's a guide based on data from the last decade:

Rating	K/BB
Excellent	4.00
Great	3.20
Above Average	2.80
Average	2.50
Below Average	2.20
Poor	1.90
Awful	1.50

HR/FB (Home Run to Fly Ball Rate)

This is the rate at which home runs are hit against a pitcher for every fly ball allowed. So if a pitcher allows 10 fly balls in a given game and one of them clears the wall, his HR/FB rate for that game is 10 percent.

This stat can fluctuate widely for a given pitcher from year to year, and that's the point of tracking it. If a pitcher has an especially high HR/FB rate one year, he might have experienced some bad batted-ball luck, which is due to turn around the following year.

Here's the FanGraphs rule of thumb for HR/FB rates:

Rating	HR/FB
Excellent	5.0
Great	7.0
Above Average	8.5
Average	9.5
Below Average	10.5
Poor	11.5
Awful	13.0

LOB% (Left On Base Percentage)

No, this isn't On-Base Percentage strictly for lefties. This is the percentage of baserunners a pitcher strands over the course of a season. This can give you an idea of how effective a pitcher has been in getting out of jams (so it's helpful when looking at relievers in particular). But the stat functions best as a predictor of sorts. Most pitchers tend to hover around the league average in LOB%, so an extremely high or low LOB% could be an indicator that a pitcher is due for regression or better success in the future.

Here's the FanGraphs guide on LOB%:

Rating	LOB%
Excellent	80
Great	78
Above Average	75
Average	72
Below Average	70
Poor	65
Awful	60

IRS% (Inherited Runs Scored Percentage)

No, IRS% is not the percentage of successful audits by the Internal Revenue Service. This stat tells us how effective a reliever has been at putting out fires he didn't create. It's the percentage of inherited runners who come around to score against him.

While some relief situations are trickier than others (entering with a runner on first and two outs is a lot easier than entering with a runner on third and no outs), the game's better relievers tend to have a lower IRS% over the course of a season:

Rating	IRS%
Excellent	20
Great	25
Above Average	28
Average	30
Below Average	33
Poor	38
Awful	40

DRS (DEFENSIVE RUNS SAVED) AND UZR (ULTIMATE ZONE RATING)

What they are: *Measurements of a player's entire defensive performance, based on how many runs he conceivably prevented from crossing the plate.*

What they are not: *DRS is not the plural for doctors, and UZR is not a form of machine gun.*

How they are calculated: *Both stats use data provided by the company Sports Info Solutions (SIS), which charts where each ball is hit. If a center fielder makes a sprinting catch on a fly ball, and the SIS data says similar fly balls get caught 60 percent of the time, the center fielder gains 0.4 points for the difficulty. If he doesn't make the play, he loses 0.6 points. At the end of the day, the player's overall score gets adjusted to the league average, then adjusted again for how many runs the adjusted score is worth.*

Why they matter: *Because error counts doled out by scorekeepers in the press box barely tell us anything about what makes a successful defender. DRS and UZR are better approximations of defensive value, as they include elements such as range, efficiency on double-play chances, and first-step quickness.*

Where you can find them: *Baseball Reference and FanGraphs.*

For decades, the only defensive evaluations readily available to us were pretty much indefensible.

There was the error—the most capricious and arbitrarily (and often unfairly) applied statistic in all of professional sports. The error, which of course generates fielding percentage, tells us not what happened but what an observer of the game felt *should* have happened. And its uselessness is matched only by its unreliability, because, on a given day, a play ruled an error in one ballpark could very well be ruled a hit in another.

On the other end of the spectrum, you have putouts and assists. These are straightforward accounts of what happened. The shortstop fielded a grounder and tossed the ball to first to throw out the runner? He gets an assist. The first baseman received the throw cleanly? He gets a putout. The morality play associated with the error was thankfully absent, but, alas, the pointlessness was present, because putout and assist totals were matters of circumstance (i.e., where the ball is put in play) rather than ability.

What about Gold Glove counts? Surely you don't get those by accident, right? Well, Rafael Palmeiro of the Texas Rangers won the award, presented annually by Rawlings, at first base in 1999 despite playing just 28 games at the position. So . . . uh . . . maybe you do?

"I laughed when I heard about it," Palmeiro told the *Dallas Morning News.*

Kind of hard to trust an award so subjective that it can elicit laughter even from the guy who receives it.

And there was the final, undocumented means of evaluating D—the ol' eye test. You know that one. If you saw a guy make a sensational diving grab on the "Web Gems" segment on ESPN's *Baseball Tonight,* he had to be a sensational defender, right? Never mind that he might have made the catch anyway with more efficient route running that wouldn't have necessitated the dive in the first place.

Obviously, those evaluation "methods" (using the word generously) persist to exist. And defense is, admittedly, the most difficult element of baseball to put to a number.

But if the aim is to evaluate players' defensive performance relative to their peers (and it ought to be), we can do a heck of a lot better than errors, putouts, assists, Gold Gloves, and the eye test. We can turn to DRS and UZR.

Fielders who have the ability to make more plays and record more outs are better than players who make fewer players and fewer outs. That's the root of what DRS and UZR set out to accomplish. Forget about dives, spins, leaps, and other superficial stuff. How many plays did this fielder make? And how many plays would the average fielder at his position make, given the same distribution of batted balls? Compare one number to the other and you see how the player fares relative to the league average.

Simple. But of course, as we've seen with so many other stats in this book, to get to simple, you've got to involve the complicated.

That's where Sports Info Solutions, originally founded as Baseball Info Solutions, comes into play. The company was founded by John Dewan, a Bill James disciple who left his career as an actuary to pursue his passion for compiling and analyzing baseball stats. Dewan and fellow programming sabermetrician Dick Cramer teamed up to make STATS LLC, a leading producer of real-time and advanced stats. After that company was sold to FOX Sports in 2000, Dewan started SIS as a means of trying to solve the perhaps unsolvable riddle of defensive metrics. SIS uses an army of video scouts to chart an exhaustive number of details, including pitch-charting and defensive positioning from every game, and sells information compiled by its database to teams, media outlets, and fantasy baseball websites.[7]

SIS records the direction, distance, speed, and type of every batted ball in every game. From there, a plus/minus scoring system

---

7 The year after the Red Sox began purchasing data from SIS, they won the World Series for the first time in eighty-six years. I'm not saying, I'm just saying.

can be formed. If, say, a shortstop makes a play on a slow roller to the hole between short and third and even one other shortstop has missed that play at some other time, he will get credit. If he misses that play and even one other shortstop has made it at some other time, he loses credit. When you add up all the credits a given fielder gained or lost over the course of a season, you get his plus/minus number.

There are other factors that go into a DRS and UZR calculation, and the two stats have a slight difference in how they are compiled and calculated.[8] DRS is a little more nuanced in terms of how good fielding plays earn extra credit and bad ones get docked. And prior to the 2020 season, DRS was fine-tuned by SIS to isolate positioning (which is dictated by the team) from the player's individual skill sets (such as range and throwing) to provide a more accurate score. That's why I, for one, lean more on DRS in my writing. But for all intents and purposes, these two stats accomplish similar objectives.

So with DRS and UZR, a score of zero is exactly average. With that in mind, here's the FanGraphs rule of thumb for both of these stats.

Rating	DRS or UZR
Excellent	+15
Great	+10
Above Average	+5
Average	0
Below Average	-5
Poor	-10
Awful	-15

---

8   DRS is the flagship stat of SIS, while statistician Mitchel Lichtman calculates UZR for FanGraphs with the use of SIS data.

Why should we look at DRS or UZR instead of error counts? Well, let's turn to the case of Josh Donaldson.

From 2013 to 2015, Donaldson, playing for the Oakland A's and then the Toronto Blue Jays, made a grand total of 57 errors—10 more than any other American League third baseman. But in that same span, he was second only to the electric Manny Machado in DRS and UZR.

Machado rightly won the AL Gold Glove at third in 2013 and '15, but in 2014 he missed half the season with a knee injury and there was an opening for somebody else to step in and nab the award. When the MLB Network crew was discussing Gold Glove candidates near the end of that '14 season, former major leaguer and now analyst Harold Reynolds, taking note of a Donaldson error count that would finish at 23 that season, said, "I'm going to throw up if he wins the Gold Glove."

When the Gold Glove announcements were made, Donaldson didn't fetch it, so Reynolds didn't retch it. The honor went to the Seattle Mariners' Kyle Seager.

But with all due respect to Reynolds and his—*ahem*—intestinal fortitude, there was nothing especially nauseating about Donaldson's Gold Glove case. Donaldson had ranked first among AL third basemen in DRS with a +20 mark. Seager was second at +10. Seager was slightly ahead of Donaldson in UZR, 8.7 to 7.9, but that is not, in all likelihood, why he won the Gold Glove. He won it because the voters, made up of managers and coaches from around the league, were looking at the situation the same way Reynolds did.

Seager, after all, had made only eight errors and was first in fielding percentage.

Now, were the 23 errors an issue for Donaldson? Yes, of course they were. You don't make that many without it counting as a blemish. Donaldson's biggest issue was with his throws, as they accounted for a ghastly 17 of his errors. He might make a fantastic diving stop of a scorching grounder, then rush his throw to get the lead runner at second, and the ball would wind up bouncing into right field.

That, though, is the beauty of DRS and UZR. Those video scouts in the SIS lab? They saw those throws, and they accounted for them. That Donaldson still managed to post strong DRS and UZR marks in spite of the errors was a testament to his elite range; his ability to get to balls others couldn't get to.

DRS and UZR didn't ignore the bad in Donaldson, but fielding percentage had ignored the good. That's an error in and of itself.

Though they are obvious improvements over past means of measuring D, these metrics are not perfect. Small sample sizes (after all, a fielder only has so many balls actually hit to him) can inflate or deflate the data, and measurements can be made incorrectly.

Then again, show me a perfect baseball stat. It doesn't exist. In considering the broadest possible range of plays (that is, all of them) and informing us how valuable a given player's contribution is relative to the average, DRS and UZR are the equivalent of cleanly fielded plays when compared to the botched attempts of old.

An A+ in D

Adrián Beltré's 477 career homers, 3,166 hits, and 116 OPS+ would have made him a solid candidate for the Hall of Fame when he becomes eligible on the 2024 ballot (he retired after the 2018 season).

But when you add his defense to the equation, Beltré's a shoo-in for selection. FanGraphs has sortable DRS and UZR data going back to 2002, and, as of this writing, the player with the highest career totals in both categories in that timespan (from any position, mind you) is Beltré, with a 222 DRS and 179 UZR.

MISCELLANEOUS DEFENSE STATS

While DRS and UZR are—for now, at least—the best total means of evaluating an individual player's defensive effort, this is very much an evolving area with increasingly sophisticated stats. Here are some other defensive metrics you should get a glove on.

OAA (Outs Above Average)

Based off Statcast's Catch Probability calculations and available at BaseballSavant.com, this is a range-based metric that shows how many outs an outfielder has saved over his peers, accounting for not only the number of plays he makes (or doesn't) but also their rate of difficulty. The radar technology used by Statcast gives a precise measurement of how far the fielder traveled to get to the ball and how much time he had to get there. So, in that sense, OAA is a step beyond the video scouting or zone-based DRS and UZR.

Prior to 2020, OAA was limited only to outfielders. But the infield numbers are now available, making this a more useful—and influential—metric when comparing defenders.

It also accounts for infield shifts. So, for instance, a particular third baseman may accrue some of his OAA while lined up in the traditional hot corner area and some while temporarily shifted to the shortstop area. You can view his OAA at each spot.

Outs Above Average

Rating	OAA
Excellent	+10 and Up
Great	1 to 9
Average	0
Poor	-1 to -9
Awful	-10 and Under

UZR/150

Because UZR is a counting stat (like homers or RBIs), this rate version that scales it to a 150-game basis can be helpful when comparing players with different amounts of playing time. It can be found on the player pages and league leaderboards at FanGraphs.

Inside Edge Fielding

Inside Edge is a sports analytics and data capture company that uses a blend of scouting and statistics to review every fielding chance for every player and put it in one of six categories, based on the difficulty of the play and the percentage of fielders at the same position who could be counted on to make the play.

Rating	IEF
Routine	90%–100%
Likely	60%–90%
About Even	40%–60%
Unlikely	10%–40%
Impossible	0%

The Inside Edge data, which is available and sortable at FanGraphs, shows which percentage of plays in those categories the player made. And unlike UZR and DRS, the Inside Edge team doesn't assign run values to the play (so the game situation—i.e., the number of outs or baserunners are involved—doesn't affect how the play is graded).

Total Zone

This data, designed and calculated by Sean Smith and provided by Baseball Reference, is good for evaluating the defense of players whose careers preceded the availability of the direct observational study SIS has been compiling this century.

Smith used different methods to analyze defense depending on the play-by-play data available and determined the number of runs above or below average the player was worth based on the number of plays made.

A different guy named Smith—Ozzie Smith—compiled 239 Total Zone Runs. That doesn't rate No. 1 all time for shortstops (Mark Belanger has 241), but it does paint him in a better light than his fielding percentage. Legendary Baltimore Orioles third baseman Brooks Robinson is tops all time at any position, with 293 Total Zone Runs.

DEF (Defensive Runs Above Average)

This stat, provided by FanGraphs, takes DRS and UZR to another level by adding in a positional adjustment that allows you to compare defensive values across positions at different baselines.

Think of it this way: A left fielder's DRS and UZR tell you his value relative to other left fielders. So the best defensive left fielder might have a similar score as the best defensive shortstop. But shortstop is a fundamentally more demanding defensive position. DEF accounts for this and tells you the player's overall defensive value to his team.

dWAR (Defensive Wins Above Replacement)

This is Baseball Reference's Wins Above Replacement calculation specifically for defense. Similar to DEF, it includes a positional adjustment and provides a total value relative to the average defender.

We'll dive deeper into the concept of WAR in Section 5.

SECTION 4:
There Is an Eye on Team—The Best Ways to Evaluate a Ballclub

In earlier chapters, I analyzed the blemishes of batting average, elucidated the ill elements of errors, and basically called the win a loser of a stat.

But, believe it or not, there is an old-school number that holds up well in the modern game. It has been around since the 1800s, is not complex to calculate, and is as important today as it has ever been.

It's called winning percentage. And, when all is said, done, and counted up, it's the stat that matters most; the stat that either puts a team into October or out of commission.

So maybe that's the only team stat we need. But in this section, we're going to look at some ways to assess a squad that delve into areas like strength of schedule and team defense. We'll also look at the numbers which make tracking single games or playoff races a little more mathematically amusing.

DIFF (RUN DIFFERENTIAL)

What it is: *A cumulative team statistic that combines offensive and defensive scoring.*

What it is not: *The part of a car's powertrain system that allows the wheels to rotate at different speeds.*

How it is calculated: *Diff = Runs Scored - Runs Allowed*

Example: *1954 Cleveland Indians*

Runs Scored	*Runs Allowed*
746	*504*

746 - 504

The 1954 Cleveland Indians' Run Differential was +242.

Why it matters: *Because within a given season, a team's winning percentage alone might not tell the entire story about their quality of play.*

Where you can find it: *MLB.com, ESPN.com, Baseball Reference, and FanGraphs all have Run Differential on their standings pages.*

At the NBA arena in my hometown of Cleveland, where some guy named LeBron James used to make a living, they came up with what can only be described—with tongue firmly planted in cheek—as "The Most Important Information Innovation of the Twenty-First Century."

It's called "The Diff," and it's a scoreboard feature that saves fans from the deep and distressing duty of trying to figure out how many points one team is ahead of the other. If the Cavaliers are up 97–92, the Diff is +5. If they are trailing 89–86, the Diff is -3. In LeBron's day, the Diff was dependably cast in the Cavs' favor. I attended one game in which Cleveland's lead was so large that one onlooker was heard to remark, "I haven't seen a Diff that large since my divorce!"

Then LeBron left town (again), and it made a big, um, Diff-erence.

Does the Diff facilitate fans' in-arena experience or insult their intelligence? Probably a bit of both. But as easy as the Diff was to criticize when it first came out, it ultimately settled into a charmed existence as a lovably quirky local specialty. You can have a good laugh at the Diff, even if you don't really need its computation cooperation to understand the score.

If the necessity of the Diff is questionable (at best) in basketball, it would be especially superfluous in baseball, unless you find those 5–2s, 10–7s, and 1–0s impossible to process without the help of your iPhone calculator.

But a different sort of Diff does have value in telling the story of a season. When you compile all the individual Diffs of a 162-game schedule into a single Diff, you have, at any given point in the season, a means of adding constructive—and sometimes crucial—context to won-lost totals.

While it is true that there is no difference, practically, between a win by 10 runs and a win by one run (either way, it's a single win in the standings), there is a strong correlation between Run Differential and won-lost record over the course of a 162-game season.

This concept actually dates all the way back to an August 2, 1954, edition of *Life* magazine, in which Branch Rickey—the visionary who signed Jackie Robinson to play for the Dodgers, created the framework for the modern minor-league farm system, and introduced the batting helmet to baseball—penned an article titled "Goodby [sic] to Some Old Baseball Ideas." Rickey wrote of a new formula for measuring team performance that, in his opinion, was "the most disconcerting and at the same time the most constructive thing to come into baseball in my memory."

The formula, designed by statistician Allan Roth, was as follows . . .

Wait, take a deep breath before reading this . . .

OK, here we go:

((Hits + Walks + Hit By Pitch/At Bats + Walks + Hit By Pitch) + (3 x [Total Bases - Hits]/4 x At Bats) + (Runs/Hits + Walks + Hit By Pitch)) - ((Hits Allowed/At Bats + (Walks Allowed + Hit By Pitch / At Bats + Walks Allowed + Hit By Pitch) + (Earned Runs Allowed / Hits Allowed + Walks Allowed + Hit By Pitch) - (Strikeouts / 8 x [At Bats + Walks Allowed + Hit By Pitch])) = G

Whoa, that's a lot of stuff. And it is fascinating to look back and see how many of the concepts that are still (necessarily) described as "advanced" in this book were being touted by Rickey and Roth before the advent of color television. Peer at this long enough and, if it doesn't break your brain, you'll see the seeds of On-Base Percentage (OBP) and Isolated Power (ISO) in the top half of the equation.

In short, Roth and Rickey were on to something. The first half of the equation is related to a team's offense, the latter part defense, with G described in the article as a team's "efficiency." So what it all boils down to is this: You want the top half to exceed the bottom half.

As tends to be the case with this stuff, we get entangled in integers to come to a very simple conclusion: You want to score more runs than you give up. What Rickey and Roth were doing was trying to identify all the elements that lead to run production and run prevention, and that effort probably should have been more appreciated in 1954.

But there's nothing wrong with the quick and dirty method of just letting the run totals speak for themselves. That's what Run Differential does.

The 2018 Seattle Mariners are an excellent recent example of Diff's predictive value within a season. When play concluded on June 13 that year, the Mariners were 44–24 and in first place in the American League West, a half-game ahead of the defending world champion Houston Astros. Even if the division lead wasn't built to last (and we know now that it surely wasn't), at least the Mariners had those two wild-card spots to lean back on. The Mariners had played 42 percent of their season schedule, so their success did not necessarily appear to be some early season fluke or hallucination. And in Seattle, specifically, this was a big deal. This was, after all, the team with the longest playoff drought in American professional sports.

But two groups of people understood that the Mariners were on shaky ground.

The first group was Mariners fans, because, well, going darn near two decades without an October berth has a way of training you to expect the worst.

The second group was Diff devotees.

In accruing that 44–24 record, the M's had scored 303 runs while allowing 276, for a Run Differential of +27.[1] That's better than a negative differential, of course, but it's not exactly the mark you'd expect from a first-place club that deep into the season. The Mariners had beaten the system, so to speak, by winning an inordinate number of close games. They were 21–9 in one-run games, 8–2 in two-run games, and 6–0 in extra-inning games.

---

1   To put that in perspective, the second-place Astros, who were 44–25 at that point in the season, had a Run Differential of +138.

Their 29–11 record (.725 winning percentage) in games decided by two or fewer runs was on pace to be the greatest in the history of the sport, bettering the record set by the 1954 Indians, who went 48–19 (.716) in such games.

It sure seemed unlikely the Mariners would be able to keep up that pace of positivity going into the second half of the season.

To further understand this, we use the Pythagorean Theorem of Baseball. This is yet another Bill James creation that uses runs scored and runs allowed to relay what a team's winning percentage *should* be. The formula for the Pythagorean Theorem is as follows:

$$W\% = [(\text{Runs Scored})^2] / [(\text{Runs Scored})^2 + (\text{Runs Allowed})^2]$$

For the 2018 Seattle Mariners, at that moment, the Pythagorean Theorem called for a .523 winning percentage. Considering the club had played 68 games, that meant that the Run Differential suggested this should have been a 36–32 team, not a 44–24 team. So, had the Mariners' record been reflective of their Run Differential, they would have been four games over .500 and not 20. Instead of being at the top of the AL West, they would have been just two games ahead of the Oakland A's in the race for the second wild-card spot.

Sure enough, the Mariners' luck ran out as the season progressed. They lost a one-run game on June 14 to fall out of first place for good. And then, over the course of the next month and a half, they watched their wild-card lead dwindle. The A's caught them on August 1, took over the lead for the second wild-card spot the following day, and never looked back. The Mariners wound up finishing 89–73, 14 games back in the AL West and eight back in the wild-card race. For the season, they were outscored 711–677, so their actual winning percentage of .549 was still worlds better than what the Pythagorean model suggested it should be (.475). But the math had caught up with them enough to prolong their playoff deprivation.

We have seen some teams defeat the Diff and get into October with less-than-inspiring Run Differentials. The 2007 Arizona D-backs, 1997 San Francisco Giants, 1987 Minnesota Twins, and 1984 Kansas City Royals all managed to win their divisions despite getting outscored by their opponents over the course of the regular season. Heck, the '87 Twins even won it all, making them the only team to do so after posting a negative regular-season Diff.

Sometimes teams have a certain magic, a certain late-inning flair that they manage to maintain over the course of a full season. We saw that recently with the 2016 Texas Rangers, who finished first in the AL West despite just a +8 Run Differential. That team posted the best winning percentage in one-run games in the modern era, with a .766 mark (36–11).

Alas, the magic rarely lasts. The Rangers went from having the best-ever record in one-run games in 2016 to the majors' worst record in one-run games in 2017 (13–24). They finished 23 games back in the West that season.

Yes, the Diff might be a silly scoreboard component in a certain NBA arena. But in baseball, it can tell us a lot about where a club is headed.

Diff-erence of Opinion

The 1927 New York Yankees had a lineup nicknamed "Murderers' Row," with Babe Ruth and Lou Gehrig combining for 107 homers and 307 runs scored. The '27 Yanks went 110–44, swept the Pirates in the World Series, and are quite often listed as the best team in the history of MLB.[2]

---

2 Heck, that's exactly what it says on the Wikipedia page for the '27 Yankees, so you know it's legit!

But the +376 Run Differential for the '27 Yankees is actually only the second-best all time. It's not even the best *Yankees* Run Differential of all time. That mark belongs to the '39 club that outscored its opponents by a whopping 411 runs. That 1939 season was the one that ushered in Lou Gehrig's retirement in June, and Ruth was already long gone. But an MVP year from Joe DiMaggio (184 OPS+) paced an offense that scored the most runs in MLB (967), and a fantastic year on the mound for Red Ruffing (148 ERA+) anchored a pitching staff that allowed the fewest runs in MLB (556).

The closest any team since 1939 has come to matching that Run Differential was the +309 mark posted in 1998 by—you guessed it—the Yankees.

SRS (SIMPLE RATING SYSTEM)

What it is: *A cumulative team statistic that combines offensive and defensive scoring.*

What it is not: *The Supplemental Restraint System in your car.*

How it is calculated: *SRS = Rdiff + SOS, where Rdiff is the difference between runs scored per game and runs allowed per game, and SOS (strength of schedule) is the number of runs per game the team's opponents are better (or worse) than the average major-league team.*

Example: *1990 Cincinnati Reds*

Runs Scored Per Game	Runs Allowed Per Game	SOS rating
4.3	3.7	-0.1

(4.3 - 3.7) + (-0.1)
0.6 - 0.1

The 1990 Reds' SRS was 0.5.

Why it matters: *Because it takes Run Differential a step further by incorporating the strength of schedule to give a more accurate reflection of the quality of the team in question.*

Where you can find it: *Baseball Reference's standings page.*

We have become a society of pundits with point systems. In the age of apps and websites like Yelp, Trip Advisor, and Rotten Tomatoes, it has never been easier to express our delight or disappointment in a restaurant, movie, hotel, you name it.

If you choose where to eat without exploring the opinions of 3,482 strangers, did you do your due diligence? And if you order the bouillabaisse without crafting a 900-word synopsis of its strengths and weaknesses, along with accompanying critique of the waiter's attentiveness and the décor and the quality of that little mint they left with the receipt—all topped off with your star assessment on a scale of 1 to 5—did you even really dine out? [3]

Baseball Reference has its own way of rating a product—in this case, a baseball team—that might not be as influential as the others mentioned above but does an even better job than Run Differential of looking beyond the won-lost record to assess a squad. Actually, SRS is a stat Baseball Reference's parent company, Sports Reference, uses for pro and college football, pro and college basketball, and the NHL. It was initially invented to help predict NFL games.

SRS values are often between -1.0 and +1.0, though they can extend higher or lower. The basic idea here is to predict how, in neutral conditions, a particular team would fare against a league-average team. So if, say, the Detroit Tigers have an SRS of +1.0, they would be favored to beat an average team by one run a game. If they have an SRS of -1.0, they would be projected to lose to an average team by one run a game. If they have an SRS of 0.0, they need to look in the mirror and realize they are, in fact, that average team.

By incorporating strength of schedule into the equation, SRS accounts for the obvious, which is that some divisions are simply better than others. If a built-to-win ballclub is fortunate enough to have a few rebuilding teams in its division, that's going to go a

---

3 Not to mention the picture of what's on your plate that you post on social media.

long way toward beefing up its Diff (and win total). But SRS will take that into consideration.

Even if you've never heard of or paid any attention to SRS, you understand it instinctively. You know in your head and heart that some wins are bigger and better than others, as some series are bigger and better than others. Yes, they all count the same in the standings, but if your favorite club comes out victorious against a team in contention, it's far more significant and satisfying than beating up on a last-place club. You see this in college sports all the time. If Duke's basketball team beats undefeated rival UNC, it's only one win, but it sure matters more than an early season non-conference win against Eastern Michigan.[4]

The 2003 AL and NL Central divisions both offer a good example. The Minnesota Twins claimed the AL Central title that season with a 90–72 record. The Chicago Cubs won the NL Central with two fewer victories, finishing at 88–74. The Twins had a +43 Run Differential, while the Cubs had a +41 mark.

So if the Twins had slightly more wins and a slightly higher Run Differential, they must have been the better team, right?

Well, not so fast. The Twins had the benefit of playing 19 games against the division-rival Detroit Tigers, who lost 119 games that year—one fewer than the all-time mark for modern major-league futility set by the 1962 New York Mets. The Twins took care of business in those games, going 15–4. Overall, the AL had five teams with 90 losses or more to the NL's four. With the schedule weighted so heavily toward intra-division and intra-league competition, these differences matter.

As you probably know, the Twins and Cubs didn't face each other that October, so there was no real reason to compare their

---

4 Sorry to any Eastern Michigan alums reading this, but, as an Ohio University graduate myself, I am allowed to pick on other Mid-American Conference schools.

SRS marks. But the fact that the Cubs had an SRS of 0.2 to the Twins' exactly average 0.0 does make it a little easier to understand how the supposed worse team of the two would be the one that would advance to the League Championship Series while the Twins got bounced in four games in the Division Series by the New York Yankees (who went 101–61 on the season with a Run Differential of +161 and an SRS of 1.0). The Cubs then lost that NLCS to the Florida Marlins, who might have been a wild-card team but did have a 0.5 SRS to the Cubs' 0.2. Don't blame Steve Bartman, blame SRS!

SRS gives us more argument for the 1939 Yankees as the best team ever. As previously noted, that team posted baseball's all-time best Run Differential (+411). It did get dinged for strength of schedule (a -0.3, as no other American League team reached the 90-win mark that season), but the Run Differential was outlandish enough to give the '39 club a 2.4 SRS mark that has never been topped.

The 1927 Yankees (2.1) are the only other team in history to have an SRS of at least 2.0. The 2001 Seattle Mariners, winners of 116 games, came closest, at 1.9, followed by the 1998 Yankees, at 1.8.

Admittedly, the SRS concept has more utility in professional football, where there are fewer games on the schedule (16) than in baseball. Trying to predict baseball, even with the help of this kind of math, is generally fruitless.

SRS can't account for injuries, weather, etc. However, the strength of schedule component cannot be ignored in a sport where the schedule is unbalanced. So this is just another tool in our toolbox when we look at the standings, mentally form our personal "power rankings," and try to gauge which teams might be under- or over-performing at a given moment in the season.

SRS-ly

A variation of the SRS idea that I like to consult is *Baseball Prospectus'* "Third Order Winning Percentage." This is a team's projected winning percentage based on underlying statistics and adjusted for the quality of opponents. At any given point in the season, you can go to BaseballProspectus. com, call up the Adjusted Standings page, and see how the third-order record compares to the actual record to get a feel for which clubs might have better days ahead or a potential regression on tap.

DER (DEFENSIVE EFFICIENCY RATING)

What it is: *The percentage of balls in play that a defense converts into outs.*

What it is not: *The word "the" in German.*

How it is calculated: *1 - (Hits - Home Runs) / (At Bats - Strikeouts - Home Runs + Sacrifice Hits + Sacrifice Flies)*

> **Note:** The version presented here is *Baseball Prospectus'* calculation.

Example: *2018 Oakland A's (all categories are opponent performance vs. A's pitchers)*

Hits	Home Runs	At-Bats	Strikeouts	Sacrifice Hits	Sacrifice Flies
1,303	184	5,517	1,237	23	30

1 - ((1,303 - 184) / (5,517 - 1,237 - 184 + 23 + 30))
1 - (1,119 / 4,149)

1 - 0.270

The 2018 A's DER was .730.

Why it matters: *Because assessing a team's defense simply by looking at its fielding percentage is insufficient at best, and misleading at worst.*

Where you can find it: *Baseball Reference (where it is labeled DefEff on each season's Standard Fielding page) and Baseball Prospectus (where it is labeled DE).*[5]

We've already discussed why the error is overrated and we've gone over stats such as Defensive Runs Saved (DRS) and Ultimate Zone Rating (UZR) that, while imperfect, at least give a clearer picture of how individual players have performed defensively.

But if player defense is tricky to tabulate, in part because of the growth in popularity of defensive shifting, then what does that say about team defense? You can call up team DRS and UZR numbers, which are simply a total accumulation of all the individual DRS and UZR numbers on a team, but a particularly spectacular (or terrible) defender on a club can have an outsized impact on the team tally.

For team D, it's best to keep things simple. No, not as simple as fielding percentage, because . . . c'mon, we're better than that, right? But DER is a solid means of getting to the heart of what we're trying to measure here: a defense's ability to turn batted balls into outs. Teams that do it well help their pitching staff and keep their fans from pulling their hair out. Teams that don't, well . . . let's just say rooting for a team with a bad defense might be the only thing nearly as bad as rooting for a team with a bad bullpen. Anything that breathes unnecessary life into opposing ballclubs is a bad thing, and that's what bad D does when makeable plays aren't made.

Though the defensive environment varies from year to year, here's a general idea of how to separate the defensive contenDERs from the pretenDERs:

---

5 *Baseball Prospectus'* sortable data requires a premium subscription.

Rating	DER
Excellent	.720 or above
Good	.710
Average	.700
Below Average	.690
Terrible	.680 or below

Unlike fielding percentage, DER includes range and the team's ability to make the play baked in. And the impact of defensive shifting on our understanding of how a team is performing defensively is lessened because, ultimately, all we really care about over the course of a long season is the total percentage of balls in play that became outs, no matter how you lined 'em up.

DER is particularly useful when comparing pitchers from different teams or even the same team in different seasons. If you play fantasy baseball, for instance, DER can help you decide which starting pitcher to put in your active lineup, as those in front of stronger defensive teams have a better chance of limiting runs. DER can also shed some light on large variations in pitcher and team performance from year to year, as with this example:

2015 Red Sox (78–84)
Rick Porcello: 9–15, 4.92 ERA
DER: .672

2016 Red Sox (93–69)
Rick Porcello: 22–4, 3.15 ERA (Cy Young)
DER: .707

And when it's time to argue about the Cy Young Award, DER is yet another data point to assist us.

On the ultra-close 2014 AL Cy Young ballot, for example, the vote came down to Corey Kluber of the Cleveland Indians and Félix Hernández of the Seattle Mariners. The two aces had nearly identical inning totals (236 for King Felix, 235 2/3 for Kluber), and Hernández had a slightly superior ERA (2.14 to 2.44). Obviously, there was much more to the vote than that, but, looking at those ERA marks, you can see why some people were surprised/angered to see Kluber edge Hernández in voting, with 169 vote points to Hernández's 159.

Digging deeper, there was a stark difference in the team defense played behind these pitchers. Hernández's Seattle club had a DER that was tied for the best in baseball, at .712. Kluber's Indians were, according to this stat, MLB's second-shakiest defensive club, at .673. So that undoubtedly impacted Kluber's total earned runs allowed.

Of course, much like team defenses themselves, DER isn't 100 percent reliable. If a team's pitchers allow a particularly high frequency of hard-hit balls, that team is likely to have a lower DER as those balls are simply more likely to wind up as hits. So, just as DER can influence the pitchers' ERAs, the pitchers themselves can influence DER.

It's like life itself. We're all in this thing together, folks.

But given a large enough sample of games, any concerns over DER are mitigated by its sheer utility and certainly by the vast improvement over fielding percentage that it provides.

Won-DER-ful

If you subscribe to *Baseball Prospectus*, you can go next level with the sortable DER data. Their website provides not just overall team DER but also DER percentages broken down by fly balls, grounders, liners, and pop-ups.

Best of all, you can find DER adjusted for ballpark tendencies, with a stat called "Park Adjusted Defensive Efficiency" (PADE). This is nice because, as we'll discuss in the next section, the ballpark affects everything. And, after all, who doesn't like getting PADE? (Sorry.)

WP (WIN PROBABILITY)

What it is: *A statistical expression of a team's chances of winning a particular game at a specific point in that game.*

What it is not: *The likelihood that a strong breeze will blow (that's Wind Probability).*

How it is calculated: *By comparing the current game situation—with the score, inning, number of outs, men on base, and run-scoring environment all taken into consideration—to comparable situations in the past, in order to arrive at a team's percentage chance of winning that game.*

Why it matters: *Because it provides historical context to specific in-game situations.*

Where you can find it: *On any day of the season, Baseball Savant's Gamefeed feature and FanGraphs' Live Scoreboard show each team's Win Probability at a given moment. Baseball Reference lists the Win Probability data of every play in every available box score going back to 1914.*

The 2016 US presidential election did . . . not go as expected. And it had a lot of people talking about the faultiness and unreliability of projection models.

Nate Silver was the renowned statistician who got his start as a baseball analyst (developing the PECOTA system that forecasts player performance) before correctly predicting the winner of all

50 states (and the District of Columbia) in the 2012 presidential race between Barack Obama and Mitt Romney. He gave Hillary Clinton a 71 percent chance of winning the presidency. The *New York Times* had her odds of winning at 84 percent. The Princeton Election Consortium took it a step further, at 95 to 99 percent. All of these sources had studied the state and national polls and used the most advanced analytical modeling techniques available.

And then Donald Trump won.

Beyond the ramifications that electoral outcome had on the country at large in terms of policy, the various academics and journalists who had built these models performed some necessary self-assessments to determine why their election odds came out the way they did. The models had varying degrees of reliability (Silver's model might have favored Clinton, but it was actually an outlier in terms of the odds of winning that it gave to Trump, essentially 30 times the chances the Princeton model did). But they all were based on national and state polls that actually weren't as far off as you might think. Trump outperformed his national polls by only 1 or 2 percentage points, and he exceeded the average swing state poll by only 2 to 3 points. One key problem is that the polls could not account for the unexpected: undecided voters who made up their minds in the final hours, voters who changed their opinions as major news events unfolded, turnout among Trump's voters being higher than anybody anticipated, etc.

So while the probability models didn't accurately predict the winner of the race, it would be wrong to call them worthless. If anything, they put a number to Trump's achievement of shocking the electoral system. They illustrated what an unexpected win it was.

In baseball, we have a stat that provides a similar service—on a daily basis, no less. It's a stat that, much like the 2016 prediction models, wouldn't always lead you to accurately guess the winner if you called it up in-game. It would, however, in the aftermath, serve as a storyteller of sorts.

Win Probability, also known as Win Expectancy, is a provider of perspective. Nothing more, nothing less. You might watch your favorite club rally to win in the bottom of ninth and think, "Boy, that was a crazy game!" This stat will tell you just how crazy it really was.

For instance, if you thought Donald Trump was an unlikely winner in 2016, how about the St. Louis Cardinals in 2011?

At the risk of further traumatizing any Texas Rangers fans reading this, let's revisit Game Six. The Rangers, up 3–2 in the best-of-seven series, were leading, 7–5, with two outs and two strikes on David Freese, with two aboard in the ninth ... and were almost certain to win their first World Series championship in franchise history.

How certain?

Well, according to WP, the Rangers' chances of winning that game in that moment were 91.8 percent. In World Series history, only three previous teams trailing in the eighth inning or later of a Game Six had rallied to win. None had done so when down to their final strike.

So when Freese punched a Neftalí Feliz pitch to the right-field corner, over the outstretched glove of Nelson Cruz for the bases-clearing triple that tied the tilt, it was statistically improbable—but obviously not impossible. And on that one iconic play, the Cardinals' chances of winning shot up 61.9 percent.

From there, the WP chart for the rest of that game looked like the kind of rollercoaster you'd have to sign a waiver to ride at Six Flags.

Cardinals catcher Yadier Molina flied out to end the ninth and make it, statistically, a 50/50 tossup, as you might expect. A hobbled Josh Hamilton hit a two-run homer in the 10th to give the Rangers a 9–7 lead and push their odds of winning back up to 92.3 percent. Then, in the bottom of the 10th, Jon Jay singled to put two runners aboard for the Cards and improve their odds to 31.7 percent. Lance Berkman then drove in the tying run with a single later that inning to push the Cards up to 63.4 percent. The Rangers were able to get out of the inning, which brought it back to 50/50. And, finally, Freese hit his game-ending leadoff shot in the bottom of the 11th to improve the Cardinals' chances of winning the game to . . . (checks notes) . . . 100 percent! They'd ride that momentum to a Game Seven win and their franchise's eleventh championship.

"If you told somebody about this game," Cruz said afterward, "they would not believe you."

Though Freese's triple was a glorious game-changer, it is not the World Series play with the largest documented effect on WP. You might be able to guess this, but that play belongs to Kirk Gibson, whose heroic limp-off homer off Dennis Eckersley in Game One in 1988 rescued a Dodgers team that, prior to his surprise pinch-hit appearance, had just a 13 percent chance of winning that game against the A's. That's why Vin Scully uttered the classic call, "In a year that has been so improbable, the impossible has happened . . . an 87-percent rise in Win Probability!"[6]

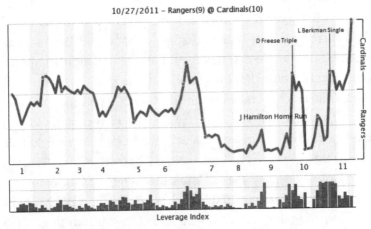

10/27/2011 – Rangers(9) @ Cardinals(10)

FanGraphs Win Probability from Game Six of the 2011 World Series. (courtesy of FanGraphs.com)

---

6 Editor's note: It's possible—even probable—that Vin didn't really say that last part.

WP is particularly worth understanding because it is the basis for Win Probability Added (WPA)—a stat that conveys each player's impact on his team's odds of winning a game by measuring the change in Win Probability from before and after a particular plate appearance. We'll cover that stat in depth within Section 5.

Odds Behavior

If you like looking at Win Probability to see how a single game might turn out, why not go the distance and see the probabilities for how an entire season will turn out?

I know, I know. Las Vegas has provided those kinds of odds for decades.

But if you want an algorithm-based perspective, FanGraphs and *Baseball Prospectus* both have playoff and World Series odds updated each and every day of the season. They come with no promises (so, uh, don't bet your mortgage on them), but they do get adjusted as results and injuries unfold, making them quite useful. And it's always fun to see a team has, say, 0.1 percent odds of winning a wild-card spot and summon your inner Jim Carrey: "So you're telling me there's a chance. YEAH!"[7]

---

7 Actually, when the 2019 Washington Nationals started out 19–31, FanGraphs was giving them just a 1.6 percent chance of winning the World Series at that point. You know what happened from that point.

MN (MAGIC NUMBER)

What it is: *A determination of how close a team is to making the playoffs or winning its division.*

What it is not: *An abbreviation for Minnesota.*

How it is calculated: *MN = Games Remaining + 1 - (Losses by second-place team - losses by first-place team)*

> **Note:** If a new second-place team emerges, the Magic Number must be adjusted to that new second-place team. The second-place team, in terms of total losses, is always used as the barometer for the first-place team's Magic Number.

Example: *National League standings, entering September 1, 1951*

Brooklyn Dodgers: 82–45, 27 games remaining
New York Giants: 76–53, 7 games back, 25 games remaining

27 + 1 - (53 - 45)
28 - 8

The Dodgers' Magic Number entering September 1, 1951, was 20.[8]

The inverse of the Magic Number is the Elimination Number. So the Giants' Elimination Number, at that time, was also 20.[9]

---

8 Spoiler: They never did get that number down to zero.
9 Double spoiler: Neither did they.

Why it matters: *Because it simplifies the math of the pennant chase and makes for a fun—or, for fans of the second-place club, frustrating—countdown.*

Where you can find it: *The MLB.com standings page, late in the season.*

Many of the "Yogi-isms" rightly or wrongly attributed to Yogi Berra (who once said, "I never said most of the things I said") were oddly profound, utterly pointless, or, quite often, equal parts of each.

"When you come to a fork in the road, take it" was not just a disconcerting direction to his Montclair, New Jersey, home; it was life advice worthy of a graduation commencement speech. "Ninety percent of the game is half mental" is a sage enough summation of the sport to absolve itself of its lack of mathematical acuity. "I want to thank everybody for making this day necessary" might be mangled phrasing, yet it's also magnificently modest.

Ah, but the best of Yogi's unusual utterances might have been, "It ain't over till it's over." On the one hand, this phrase is redundant. In the strictest linguistic sense, it is like saying, "It is what it is," or "Blueberries are blueberries." When taken literally, it is devoid of actual insight; a statement of the obvious.

And yet somehow, "It ain't over till it's over" has a beautiful sense of hope attached to it. Though short of informational, it is inspirational. It is a reminder of the punch-yourself-out-of-the-corner possibility of the human spirit.

Before it was a Lenny Kravitz song or a line in *Rocky Balboa*— the Sylvester Stallone vehicle that brought back the fictional boxing world's most indefatigable fighter—"It ain't over till it's over" was how Berra described the 1973 playoff race. He was manager of the New York Mets who were, in his own inimitable words, "overwhelming underdogs." The Mets were in last place as late as August 30, 6 1/2 games behind the first-place St. Louis Cardinals in the tightly packed National League East. But they stormed back in September and wound up finishing in first, 1 1/2 games ahead of the Cards.

Would "It ain't over till it's over" be so widely cited and employed today if Berra's Mets had not mounted such a comeback? As prominent a public figure as Berra was, it's a point worth pondering. That the phrase's utility as a squad-inspirer—especially when accompanied by Tug McGraw's "Ya gotta believe!" motto—was instantly proven undoubtedly added to its allure.

All Berra was doing, ultimately, was telling us what the Magic Number tells us. Forget what they say about the stereotypically overweight sopranos of the opera. It ain't over till the Magic Number—and by extension the Elimination Number[10]—says so. And when we get into the home stretch of the major-league season, the standings page at MLB.com lays out the MNs and the Es quite clearly. For fans of an October-bound ballclub, there is nothing more satisfying than those days when, either by head-to-head combat or outcomes in separate cities, you get to subtract two from the MN and continue to close in on a clincher.

That brings up another pointed question: When is it appropriate to begin counting the Magic Number down? To each his own, of course, but my personal opinion would be . . . never! If, say, the Baltimore Orioles are the only AL East team to win on Opening Day and everybody else is 0–1, their Magic Number to clinch the division is 161.

Tug was right. Ya gotta believe!

But as a native Clevelander, I remember the Magic Number being of particular citywide importance in the late summer of 1995, when the Indians were nailing down their first October berth since 1954 by dismantling the rest of the AL Central in that strike-shortened, 144-game season. Under those specific

---

10 Listed under E# on the MLB.com standings page.

circumstances—the drought profound and the conclusion fore-gone—to peek at the Magic Number as early as the All-Star break (when, for the record, it was 67) was not unreasonable.

The Magic Number can also lend a layer of context to situations where the magic runs out—as in that above-cited NL pennant race in which the Dodgers were run down by a red-hot Giants team that wound up forcing a three-game playoff capped by Bobby Thomson's "Shot Heard 'Round the World" and Russ Hodges's famous radio declaration, "The Giants win the pennant! The Giants win the pennant! The Giants win the pennant! The Giants win the pennant!"

Magic.

Ta-da!

The first known usage of the Magic Number came during the 1947 pennant race between the New York Yankees and Boston Red Sox, when an article in the September 12, 1947, edition of the *Washington Post* included this in a recap of a tilt between the two teams: "The Yankees reduced the Magic Number to four. That is the combination of games the Yankees must win or the Red Sox must lose in order to ensure the flag for the Yankees."

The Yankees did, indeed, win the league pennant that year, but it was the Detroit Tigers—not the Red Sox—who finished in second place.

SECTION 5
The Full Count—Context Stats that Add Clarity

If you've made it this far, I hope that you've gotten a better understanding of the best ways to evaluate a player's offensive, defensive, or pitching prowess.

But baseball is a complicated game, replete with bizarre bounces, eccentric stadiums, and demanding duties. Hit a ball square on the barrel and you might not be rewarded. Set the world aflame all evening but then strike out with the bases loaded in the ninth and your clutchness might come into question. Drive in a run in the top of an inning but let a grounder get past your glove in the bottom and it can be hard to know if one element offset the other.

In this section, we'll cover luck, skill, and the total package. We'll salute the stats that calculate the quirks of serendipity, setting, and situation. We will then conclude by diving into the most prevalent and influential advanced metric of all—the one that attempts to wrap everything into a nice and tidy number.

BABIP (BATTING AVERAGE ON BALLS IN PLAY)

What it is: *The measure of what percentage of a batter's balls in play go for hits, or, conversely, what percentage of balls in play against a pitcher go for hits. So walks and strikeouts don't count, because they are not batted balls. And home runs don't count, because they are not in play (unless Stretch Armstrong is manning the outfield).*

What it is not: *The sound your car makes when it needs a new muffler.*

How it is calculated: *BABIP = (Hits - Homers) / (At Bats - Strikeouts - Homers + Sacrifice Flies)*

Examples: *Ichiro Suzuki, OF, 2004 Seattle Mariners*

Hits	Home Runs	At-Bats	Strikeouts	Sacrifices
262	8	704	63	3

(262 - 8) / (704 - 63 - 8 + 3)
254 / 636

Ichiro Suzuki's 2004 BABIP was .399.

Jim Palmer, RHP, 1975 Baltimore Orioles (all stats are opponent numbers)

Hits	Home Runs	At-Bats	Strikeouts	Sacrifices
253	20	1,172	193	4

(253 - 20) / (1,172 - 193 - 20 + 4)
233 / 636

Jim Palmer's 1975 opponents' BABIP was .242.

Why it matters: *Because weird things can happen when a ball is sent hurtling into the field of play. BABIP elaborates on batting average by removing outcomes not affected by the opposing defense (namely, home runs and strikeouts).*

Where you can find it: *Baseball Savant, FanGraphs, and Baseball Reference.*

It's a shame this stat was not yet widely cited at a time when a speedy second baseman named Leon Joseph "Bip" Roberts was still playing, because dips, drops, and blips in Bip's BABIP would have been a lot of fun to reference. But at least, once you read this, you'll be fully prepared the next time baseball has a Bip.

Like FIP—but applicable for both hitters and pitchers—BABIP can identify players who have had their past results affected by good or bad luck and are perhaps due for a turnaround, be it within the context of the current season or perhaps in the ensuing season. A hitter with a .360 BABIP might have benefited from good luck; a hitter with a .240 BABIP might have suffered poor luck.

An average BABIP is right around .300. Of course, there are fluctuations to this from year to year or team to team or player to player. In the first 19 seasons this century, the league average BABIP was anywhere from as low as .293 to as high as .303.

For hitters especially, there are several factors that can influence BABIP which have nothing to do with luck. Those who maintain a high line-drive rate are going to have more balls land as hits than those more prone to grounders or pop-ups. Speedy players are more likely to regularly leg out infield singles and preserve a higher BABIP than lumbering sluggers. And if you play in a hitter-friendly park like Colorado's Coors Field, this, too, can positively influence your BABIP, whereas a traditionally pitcher-friendly park like San Diego's Petco Park is going to drag it down.

But if we take .300 as a general rule of thumb, we can identify outliers that stand a decent chance of going up or down.

According to Baseball Reference, there are only 26 players who have posted a BABIP of .400 or higher in a full season in the modern era (from 1901 to the present day):

.443: Ty Cobb, 1911 Detroit Tigers
.433: Shoeless Joe Jackson, 1911 Cleveland Naps
.424: Ty Cobb, 1912 Detroit Tigers
.423: Babe Ruth, 1923 New York Yankees
.422: George Sisler, 1922 St. Louis Browns
.422: Rogers Hornsby, 1924 St. Louis Cardinals
.418: Nap Lajoie, 1901 Philadelphia Athletics
.416: George Stone, 1906 St. Louis Browns
.416: Ty Cobb, 1922 Detroit Tigers
.415: Jesse Burkett, 1901 St. Louis Cardinals
.414: Ty Cobb, 1913 Detroit Tigers
.414: Harry Heilmann, 1923 Detroit Tigers
.410: Ty Cobb, 1910 Detroit Tigers
.409: Rogers Hornsby, 1921 St. Louis Cardinals
.408: Rod Carew, 1977 Minnesota Twins
.406: Yoan Moncada, 2019 Chicago White Sox
.405: Shoeless Joe Jackson, 1912 Cleveland Naps
.404: José Hernández, 2002 Milwaukee Brewers
.403: Roberto Clemente, 1967 Pittsburgh Pirates
.403: Manny Ramirez, 2000 Cleveland Indians
.401: George Sisler, 1920 St. Louis Browns
.400: Heinie Zimmerman, 1912 Chicago Cubs
.400: Ty Cobb, 1917 Detroit Tigers
.400: Ty Cobb, 1919 Detroit Tigers
.400: Bill Terry, 1930 New York Giants
.400: Luke Appling, 1936 Chicago White Sox

Now, if you think citing that list was largely an excuse to mention a guy named Heinie, you're not totally wrong. But a couple other things stand out: Only five of these seasons came after 1936, which falls in line with the overall defensive improvement in the sport as it evolved. Also, 23 of the 26 players listed had career batting averages north of .300. So it's not especially outlandish that they would have a season (or, in the cases of Cobb, Hornsby, Jackson, and Sisler, multiple seasons) when the stars aligned.

Our guy Heinie had a .295 career average, so he's not much of an outlier, either. And as of this writing, it's too early in Moncada's career to make any real judgments on his offensive ceiling. But what the heck got into Hernández in 2002?

To be fair, José Hernández was what baseball people would call "a nice little player." He spent all or part of 15 seasons in the big leagues, playing every position other than pitcher and catcher. He was even, thanks to some late-game defensive maneuvering, kinda/sorta slotted in as the DH in two games during his career.[1]

Obviously, though, Hernández was not a guy you'd ordinarily associate with the Cobbs and Ruths and Hornsbys of the world. He made that list with the benefit of perhaps one of the luckiest seasons in baseball history.

When we dig into the advanced numbers of Hernández's 2002 season with the Brewers, we see that his line-drive rate (26 percent) was slightly north of his average for his 15-year career (22 percent), and his pop-up rate (5 percent) was a little south of his career average (9 percent). But neither of these fluctuations are enough to account for such an abnormal BABIP. Actually, Hernández put fewer balls in play, period. He put the ball in play in 61 percent of his plate

---

1   It might not surprise you to learn that the two teams which somehow found themselves having José Hernández oh-so-briefly occupy the DH role—the 1997 Chicago Cubs and 2005 Cleveland Indians—did not win the World Series.

appearances over the entirety of his career, but only 54 percent in that oh-so-magical season of 2002. In fact, Hernández struck out so frequently in '02 that Brewers manager Jerry Royster benched him eight times in the last 11 games of the season so that he would not topple Bobby Bonds's then-record for strikeouts in a season.[2]

And so, strikeouts aside, the baseball gods smiled upon Hernández in '02, and he was a first-time (and only time) All-Star as a result, which means he got to be there for the infamous mid-summer classic tie in his home park. Could it be that Bud Selig's iconic shrug was not in reference to the odd situation at hand but, in fact, a response to Hernández's unusually high batting average? Discuss among yourselves.

Bottom line for Hernández: Balls that didn't ordinarily fall in for hits fell in for hits. His abnormally high BABIP led to what was, for him, an abnormally high batting average of .288 (he had been a career .250 hitter in the 10 years prior). The following year, Hernández signed a free agent deal with the Rockies (one-year contract for $1 million), but not even the thin air of Colorado and the wide-open space of Coors Field could help him maintain that berserk BABIP. In a 2003 season in which he was dealt to the Cubs mid-year (and later the Pirates), Hernández BABIP'd a much-more-common .311, driving his real batting average all the way down to .225.

It works the other way, too, and let's apply the lesson to a pitcher: Robbie Ray. In 2016 with the Arizona D-backs, Ray had what most people would describe as a rough year. He went 8–15 with a 4.90 ERA. He struck out 218 batters in 174 1/3 innings (good!), but had a 1.47 WHIP (bad!).

A ton of factors coalesce to tell the story of a season and, for Ray in 2016, there were valid concerns about his ability to get

---

2 Hernández finished with 188, one shy of Bonds's mark from 1970. However, in the time since, 33 players have struck out more than 188 times, with 13 doing so more than 200 times (through the 2019 season).

through an opponent's order a third time and the depth of his repertoire beyond his 94-mph fastball. But sometimes the simplest explanation is the correct one: Ray's opponents had an abnormally high .355 BABIP in that '16 season. How abnormal? Well, it was tied for the fourth highest opponent BABIP on record, per Baseball Reference:

1. .362: Les Sweetland, 1930 Philadelphia Phillies
2. .358: Kevin Millwood, 2008 Texas Rangers
3. .357: Kevin Brown, 1994 Texas Rangers
4. .355: Glendon Rusch, 2001 New York Mets
   .355: Ian Snell, 2008 Pittsburgh Pirates
   .355: Robbie Ray, 2016 Arizona Diamondbacks

Heinie Zimmerman has company from Les Sweetland in the Department of Funny Baseball Names. But the important takeaway here is that Ray's chances of repeating a historically bad BABIP were pretty slim. In the 15 years prior to Opening Day 2017, not a single qualifying pitcher had repeated an opponents' BABIP of .330 or more in consecutive years. So Ray had history on his side going into the following season, and history did, indeed, prevail. Though Ray did elevate his already-impressive strikeout rate in '17 (from 28.1 percent to 32.8 percent) and did do a better job limiting line drives (from 28 to 25 percent), the decrease in balls in play falling for hits (from .352 to .270) was the biggest factor in his metamorphosis from a 15-game loser to a 15-game winner. He lowered his ERA from 4.90 to 2.89 and improved his ERA+ from 91 to 163. He was a first-time All-Star and finished seventh in the NL Cy Young voting (and could be heard screaming "BABIP, baby!" when he walked off the mound after his final inning pitched of that triumphant season).[3]

---

3 OK, that last part is not true.

And if the wily eyed among you noted that the .270 BABIP from 2017 was especially low, you're starting to catch on! In 2018, Ray regressed back to a 3.93 ERA, as his opponents' BABIP increased to a more standard .293 mark (he also got hurt, which tends to happen to pitchers these days).

So while Hernández and Ray are an especially extreme example, the lesson they provide is a valuable one: If a player's BABIP in a given season is particularly high, relative to his career norm, it's not likely to last.

BABIPidi-Bobbidi Boo

In the live ball era (since 1920), only two hitters amassed at least 10,000 plate appearances and a career BABIP of .350 or higher: Rod Carew (.359) and Derek Jeter (.350). They are evidence that a high BABIP isn't always luck; sometimes it's skill.

Carew's ability to direct the ball—as if his bat were a magic wand—was legendary. And Jeter's so-called "inside-out" swing, which allowed him to spray the ball to all fields, had an impact on a fielder's ability to judge the ball off the bat.

xBA (EXPECTED BATTING AVERAGE), xSLG (EXPECTED SLUGGING PERCENTAGE), AND xwOBA (EXPECTED WEIGHTED ON-BASE AVERAGE)

What they are: *Measurements of what statistic (be it BA, SLG, or wOBA) ordinarily would have resulted from batted balls comparable to the ones struck by the hitter or allowed by the pitcher.*

What they are not: *BAs, SLGs, or wOBAs that have quit their jobs (because that would be Ex-BA, Ex-SLG, and Ex-wOBA).*

How they are calculated: *Using Statcast technology, each batted ball is assigned an xBA, xSLG, and xwOBA based on how often comparable batted balls—in terms of Exit Velocity, Launch Angle, and, on weakly hit balls, Sprint Speed—have become hits. And then, for xSLG and xwOBA, the specific type of hits—singles, doubles, triples, and home runs—are valued the exact same way they would be for the regular SLG and wOBA calculations.*

Why they matter: *Because they give us a more statistically accurate ability to figure out, with apologies to Tina Turner, what luck's got to do, got to do with it.*

Where you can find them: *BaseballSavant.com, which is MLB.com's clearinghouse for all available Statcast data.*

The game between the Washington Nationals and St. Louis Cardinals on April 21, 2015, at Nationals Park, was compelling enough on its own. Gio González pitched six scoreless innings for the Nats, and the only moment marring Lance Lynn's 6 1/3 innings of work was the Bryce Harper groundball single that squeaked by to score an early run. Nationals closer Drew Storen blew the 1–0 save opportunity in the ninth when Matt Holliday hit a groundball single of his own to score Matt Carpenter from third. But in the bottom of the 10th, the home team had a hero in the form of Yunel Escobar, whose two-out, walk-off solo homer sent Washington fans home happy with a 2–1 victory.

But as entertaining as it might have been at the moment, this game would be an afterthought now if not for the statistical boost available on the MLB Network broadcast.

For the first time in history, not only did those watching on TV have access to the velocity readings of the ball coming out of the pitcher's hand, but also that same ball smacking off the bat. When Escobar connected with the game-winner, we had the Exit Velocity, Launch Angle, and the most accurate Projected Home Run Distance possible, thanks to the Doppler radar technology and the high-definition cameras in the building. When the Cardinals' Kolten Wong swiped second in the eighth inning, we had access to his Sprint Speed, or top running speed. When Jayson Werth hit a ninth-inning line drive in the direction of Cards center fielder Jon Jay, we had a reading of Jay's exact Distance Covered to get to the ball and how quickly he got there.

Baseball was irrevocably altered with that first broadcast featuring Major League Baseball's Statcast system. In the time since, the state-of-the-art player tracking technology has revolutionized the way we watch and discuss the sport—and even the way players play it. Statcast is directly responsible for a generation of hitters putting increased attention and emphasis on Launch Angles—which was far from the only factor in the steep rise in league-wide home-run rates but was undoubtedly a part of the equation. Statcast also inspired added emphasis on pitch Spin Rates—or revolutions per minute—with clubs now able to target possibly undervalued pitchers who weren't using their best offerings enough.

Statcast changed the game, plain and simple. Its measurements include everything mentioned above, as well as:

- *Arm Strength*: How many miles per hour a fielder throws the ball.
- *Base-to-Base Time*: How many seconds it takes a runner to get from one base to another.
- *Extension*: How far, in feet, past the mound a pitcher's release point is on a pitch.
- *Lead Distance*: How many feet a runner ranges off the bag.
- *Pitch Velocity*: A more precise measurement of the miles per hour of a particular pitch.
- *Perceived Pitch Velocity*: Taking both velocity and extension into account to quantify how fast a pitch appears to the hitter.
- *Pop Time*: How many seconds it takes a catcher to get the ball out of his glove and to the base on a stolen base or pickoff attempt.
- *Catch Probability*: The likelihood, in percent, that an outfielder will be able to make a catch on a particular batted ball, accounting for distance needed, time available, direction, and proximity to the wall.
- *Outs Above Average*: As mentioned in the Miscellaneous Defensive Stats chapter, a measure of an outfielder's skill at making plays.

I'm sure some people roll their eyes and say Statcast is too new-fangled a way of looking at this grand ol' game. But at its heart, it's actually pretty old school in that the areas Statcast is measuring are the same areas scouts have always prioritized in their reports. The difference is that our data is now more accurate and more readily available to the public . . . and that's a good thing.

All of those mentioned are worthwhile numbers to know, and Statcast's ability to help us analyze and understand defense and overall influence on the sport is only going to grow in the coming years. (That's why you're reading this book!)

But for the purposes of this book's focus on tools the average fan can use to better evaluate players, I would argue the biggest offering Statcast has afforded us so far is the ability to properly analyze who has hit (or pitched) into poor batted-ball luck.

When I was a baseball beat writer in the 2000s and early 2010s, I can't tell you how many times a manager, coach, or player would resort to some variation of the same line about a hitter who was not performing well: "He's hitting them hard, just right at people." I can't tell you how many pitchers would voice the frustration that came with bloopers, dribblers, and squibbers going for hits when they should have been outs.

And sure, there were many times it did *seem* like a particular player had more than his fair share of hard liners finding the web of the glove instead of the freedom of the grass or when a pitcher was basically betrayed by the elements. But at the time, all us writers had at our disposal to relay such analysis to our readers was the anecdotal evidence that comes with the eye test and those tired clichés coming from the clubhouse.

Now, thanks to Statcast and the information available at Baseball Savant, we don't need to trust the words of a hitter or pitcher bemoaning his bad luck. The data is available to us in the form of xBA, xSLG, and xwOBA—stats that we can utilize for hitters and pitchers alike.

All the ideas previously espoused in this book apply here, only with a little "x" involved this time. In other words, xSLG tells us more than xBA, and xwOBA tells us more than both. And the same values that apply to BA, SLG, and wOBA apply here, too. Just as .300 is considered a good BA, .300 is considered a good xBA. Just as .500 is considered a great SLG, .500 is considered a great xSLG. Just as .290 is considered a bad wOBA, .290 is considered a bad xwOBA. We already have a clear idea of "good" and "bad" batting averages in our head, but, in case it's helpful, let's revisit the rules of thumb for SLG and wOBA—this time with the little "x" included:

Rating	xSLG	xwOBA
Excellent	.550 or above	.390 or above
Great	.500	.370
Above Average	.450	.340
Average	.420	.320
Below Average	.400	.310
Poor	.390	.300
Awful	.380 or below	.290 or below

What these three "expected" stats boil down to is using quality of contact instead of actual outcomes to evaluate performance. We've shown how a stat like FIP has long aimed to accomplish exactly that. The Statcast metrics use technology to fine-tune that process (though the fact that FIP is placed on the same scale as ERA ultimately makes it more relatable) and also bring it to the batting side.

Take Seattle Mariners slugger Daniel Vogelbach as an example. Over the course of the 2017–18 seasons, Vogelbach had one of the game's worst differentials between his actual wOBA (.295) and his xwOBA (.359). If you look at the chart above, you'll see that a .295 mark rates as poor, while a .359 mark rates between above average and great. Big difference. In the first half of the 2019 season, Vogelbach's batted-ball outcomes aligned almost exactly with his quality of contact (a .373 wOBA and a .374 xwOBA), and he was a first-time All-Star.[4]

On the other end of the spectrum—in terms of role and results—there was St. Louis Cardinals right-hander Michael Wacha, who in 15 starts in 2018 had the game's highest differential between his opponents' wOBA (.286, or awful) and their xwOBA (.350, or above average), leading to an ERA+ of 121. In the 2019 season, his opponents' wOBA (.364) and xwOBA (.356) were in much greater alignment, and his ERA+ dropped to 90.

Those are examples where the expected Statcast stats perhaps had some predictive power. But to be abundantly clear, that's not always the case. These stats were designed to be *descriptive*, not predictive.

Still, a descriptive stat that shines a real light on batted-ball luck (or lack thereof) is a heck of a lot more reliable than a quote from the clubhouse. And whether it's these expected metrics or the other offerings listed above, Statcast is all about giving us the cold, hard, numeric truth.

Roll Out the Barrels

Batters have talked about barreling up the baseball for about as long as the game has been played, but Statcast has put a number to the notion.

The Barrel classification is assigned to batted balls whose comparable hit types—in terms of Exit Velocity and Launch Angle—have led to at least a .500 batting average

---

4 Vogelbach's performance did taper off in the second half. But it wasn't due to poor luck, because his wOBA and xwOBA continued to remain relatively well-aligned.

and 1.500 slugging percentage league-wide since Statcast was implemented in 2015. In a given year, depending on the offensive environment, the average Barrel result might even be better than those marks, but a .500 BA and 1.500 SLG are the baselines.

In order to be considered "Barreled," a batted ball must have an exit velocity of at least 98 mph. At that speed, balls must be struck between 26 to 30 degrees to earn the Barrel classification. For every mph over 98, the range of launch angles expands.

Remember our friend Khris Davis, who for a time was the annual owner of a measly .247 average? In the 2018 season, nobody in MLB with at least 300 batted ball events had a higher Barrels per plate appearance (10.7%) or Barrels per batted ball event (17.2%). So that's another means of understanding what a force of nature he was, batting average aside.

PARK FACTORS

What they are: *Measures of how much a ballpark's unique attributes contribute to the run-scoring environment.*

What they are not: *Scales illustrating how well or how poorly a given major-league player is at parallel parking his car.*

How they are calculated: *Different sources calculate park factors differently, but the most basic measurement is to take the total number of runs scored by Team X and its opponents in Team X's home ballpark and divide that figure by the total runs scored by Team X and its opponents in Team X's road games.*

You can do the same exercise with other stats, such as doubles, triples, homers, etc.

Example: *1962 Los Angeles Dodgers, Dodger Stadium*

Runs Scored and Allowed at Home	Runs Scored and Allowed on the Road
698	841

698 / 841

Dodger Stadium's 1962 Park Factor was 0.830, which means it strongly favored pitchers. Compare that with the Dodgers' final season at Ebbets Field in 1957, when Ebbets' Park Factor of 1.329 strongly favored hitters.

Why they matter: *Because every ballpark is different, it can be helpful to have a guide for understanding the effects a given setting is having on team run scoring.*

Where to find them: *ESPN.com, FanGraphs, Baseball Prospectus, and StatCorner.com all offer a form of park factor.*

We can quibble about the intricate differences between maple wood shades and densities on NBA floors, the atmospheric effects on playing field conditions in the NFL, or even the alterations in lighting systems from arena to arena that can impact approaches in the NHL.

But the bottom line is that, at the highest level of the sport in question, basketball courts, football fields, and ice rinks are all essentially created equal.

One of the beauties of baseball is how each of the thirty ballparks has its own dimensions, distinct from the rest. It's not just the concessions, concourses, and city skylines (or lack thereof) giving fans a sense of place, but also the fields themselves.

Sometimes the quirks are shaped by peculiarities within a given plot of land, such as Fenway Park's Green Monster arising as a means of preventing folks from getting a free look at the game from the buildings on Lansdowne Street. Or in one extreme case, a single person dictated the shape of things, as the Yankees gave old Yankee Stadium a short right-field porch to accommodate a gentleman by the name of Babe Ruth. (Pinstripe-wearing southpaw sluggers remain thankful, as the new Yankee Stadium maintained those same dimensions.)

From the essentially ancient jewel box designs of Fenway and Wrigley Field to the westward expansion that birthed Dodger Stadium and Angel Stadium to the multi-sport setups demonstrated by Oakland-Alameda Coliseum and the Rogers Centre to the retro classic phase that began with Baltimore's Camden Yards, baseball's various stadium stages are all on display in the present day. We no longer have the white ceiling of the Metrodome that once ate a Dave Kingman pop-up and generally wreaked havoc for fielders trying to track the flight of the ball. Or the movable fences that Indians maverick owner Bill Veeck temporarily brought to Cleveland Municipal Stadium. Or the hill on the warning track at Houston's Minute Maid Park that was a hamstring health risk for many a sprinting center fielder.

But there are still plenty of peculiarities in play from park to park. Asymmetrical setups are an essential element of the soul, character, and charm of baseball.

Unfortunately, they can make it pretty darn difficult to properly evaluate what you're watching.

More than in any other sport, the field itself is a distinct variable influencing outcomes in baseball. Beyond the differences in dimensions, distinctions in air quality and topology can alter the way the ball travels.

Colorado's Coors Field, for instance, is notoriously friendly to hitters because of Denver's high altitude, to the point that the Rockies installed a humidor prior to the 2002 season to keep the leather baseballs from drying out and to limit the number of long balls and (hopefully) get people to stop calling the place "Coors Canaveral." (It's still a hitter's paradise, but the humidor did help.) San Diego's Petco Park was so far on the opposite end of the spectrum, thanks in part to the marine layer that limits the flight of the ball, that the Padres moved the fences in prior to the 2013 season.

Park factors help us assess how much the ballpark contributes to the offensive success of a team or player. A 1.000 OPS season in Coors Field simply isn't the same as a 1.000 OPS season in Petco Park, and park factors help us account for that.

But there is no one true way of calculating or relaying park factors, and we could really get lost in a mess of math if we try to explain all of that. It's better to just know where to find this stuff.

Baseball Reference uses three-year park factors to provide a larger sample of data and embeds them into its calculations for ERA+ and OPS+ to figuratively put all players on the same playing field. That's why those stats are so much better at providing context than ERA and OPS themselves.

FanGraphs, meanwhile, has sortable park factors in one-year, three-year, and five-year increments, as well as type of outcome (single, double, triple, homer, strikeout, walk, ground ball, fly ball, line drive, and pop-up). All of these are adjusted to a scale where 100 is neutral. So anything higher than 100 benefits hitters and anything below 100 benefits pitchers.

You can also sort the FanGraphs Park Factor by handedness (homers for lefties, homers for righties, triples for lefties, triples for righties, etc.). This is meaningful because certain parks might only benefit specific subsets of hitters. Cleveland's Progressive Field, for example, traditionally plays much better for left-handed hitters (105 FanGraphs Park Factor in 2018, where the average is scaled to 100 instead of 1.00) than right-handed hitters (98), who have to vie with the 19-foot wall in left field.

While the impact a 19-foot wall is going to have on ballgames is a constant, a given facility's park factors can change from year to year, depending on anything from the average distance of home runs in a given season to weather patterns. In 2013, players, coaches, and broadcasters began to note that the ball wasn't carrying as well in notoriously hitter-friendly Globe Life Park in Arlington, Texas. As measured by ESPN.com, the park factor at the facility went from 1.183 in 2012 all the way down to 0.985. One reason? The team had made some updates to the area behind home plate, removing glass windows of a luxury club to provide an open-air experience for patrons. This impacted air circulation in the building and reduced the jet stream effect on fly balls to the outfield.

If you just want the quickest, simplest breakdown of how the parks are playing in a given season, I like to consult ESPN's easily searchable and sortable Park Factors list. It doesn't break things down by handedness, but it provides a basic, single-season rundown of how the thirty parks rank in terms of walks, hits, doubles, triples, homers, and runs. So at any point in the calendar, you can call it up and see which parks have favored hitters and which have favored pitchers that year. ESPN uses the same calculation presented at the top of this chapter, where 1.00 is neutral.

Just as there are not standardized dimensions in baseball field layouts, there is not a standardized means of calculating park factors. But consulting any of them lends helpful context to what you're watching.

A Walk in the Park

The Milwaukee Brewers achieved one of the great trade pickups of modern times when they landed Christian Yelich from the Miami Marlins, just in time for Yelich to morph into an MVP-worthy monster. Yelich had a career OPS of .800 when the pre-2018 trade was made, with 59 homers in 643 games. But in his first season in Milwaukee, he had a 1.000 OPS with 36 homers in 147 games.

Yelich had matured as a hitter, but the change in parks definitely played a part in his meteoric rise. He went from Marlins Park, which, according to FanGraphs, had a 92 (or 8 percent below neutral) home run Park Factor for left-handed hitters in 2017, to Miller Park, which had a 112 (or 12 percent above neutral) homer Park Factor for lefties in 2018.

WPA (WIN PROBABILITY ADDED)

What it is: *A measurement of how much a player impacted his team's chances of winning from one event to the next.*

What it is not: *The Works Progress Administration.*

How it is calculated: *The team's Win Probability before a plate appearance, stolen base, caught stealing, or pickoff is subtracted from the team's Win Probability after a plate appearance, stolen base, caught stealing, or pickoff.*

Example: *Blue Jays right fielder Joe Carter's game-winning home run to end Game Six of the 1993 World Series*

Blue Jays' Win Probability Before the Carter Homer	Blue Jays' Win Probability After the Homer
34%	100%

1.00 - 0.34

Carter's Win Probability Added for his Series-ending swat was 0.66.

Why it matters: *Because it puts events into context and relays how much impact a specific player has had on a game and, when taken cumulatively, a season. This makes it a good "story stat" and a better measure of clutch performance than a stat such as batting average with runners in scoring position.*

Where you can find it: *FanGraphs and Baseball Reference.*

Do you believe in "clutch," or do you believe in chaos?

The debate has raged in baseball and other sports for decades. Certain athletes—the well-decorated likes of Derek Jeter and Michael Jordan and Tom Brady—are said by some to be in possession of the "clutch gene," no matter how scientifically unprovable this theory may be. And you don't have to be a Hall of Famer to be blessed with this gene. Players like Édgar Rentería, Robert Horry, or David Tyree were not considered greats of their time in their respective sports, yet rose to the occasion when it mattered most. Rentería had an OPS+ below league average for his career, but he had the game-winning hit in not one, but *two* World Series clinchers. How does that happen? He must be clutch, right?!

Sabermetrically inclined individuals will tell you no, he is not. They will argue—perhaps rightly so—that given a large enough sample of games, the best players will put up the best numbers, the worst will put up the worst, and so on and so forth. They will say it's better to be lucky than good, and that Rentería, coming to bat at the right time in the right moment in the right matchup, was more the former than the latter. Give him credit for coming through and allow him to polish those rings with pride, but don't call him clutch. Call him an individual who benefited from the chaotic and highly unpredictable pinball game known as October baseball.

I'm not here to beat any particular drum in this debate. Athletes are only human, and it certainly seems that some are more unflappable in high-pressure situations than others. That has to count for something.

But at the same time, I'm not a big believer in labeling baseball players clutch or unclutch based on extremely limited numbers of plate appearances or innings pitched. David Price, despite all his regular-season accolades, had to hear for years that he didn't have what it took to pitch in the postseason. He made 11 postseason starts between Game One of the American League Division Series in 2010 and Game Two of the American League Championship Series in 2018, going winless in all of them with an unflattering 5.72 ERA. The narrative hounded him, angered him, maybe even motivated him. And a switch flipped in his second start of that '18 ALCS. He pitched six scoreless innings in a victory over the Astros in the Game Five clincher, then allowed just three runs in 13 2/3 World Series innings against the Dodgers to earn two more victories as Boston won it all.

"I hold all the cards now," he said when that Series was over. "And that feels so good. *So* good."

Evidently, Price's secret, mid-ALCS "clutch gene" implantation procedure had been successful.

The existence of "clutchness" is debatable, but the outcome of games is not.[5] And that's why we have the Win Probability Added stat. It makes no judgment on events in the past and offers no assurances of events to come. All it does is tell us how a player has impacted the outcome of games.

WPA is a huge step forward from the stats many people use to characterize clutchness. Batting average with runners in scoring position is flawed, because:

A. it involves batting average (duh); and

B. the number of opportunities won't be large enough to derive any real substance.

The most plate appearances with runners in scoring position for any player in a single season on record were the 258 for Don Baylor in 1979. That's less than half a season's worth of trips to the plate—and that's at the very top end.

---

5 Well, unless you feel your team got hosed by an umpire or referee, but that's a subject for another time.

Then, of course, there's RBI. Not only is it a lousy stat in general (as it unfairly favors those who have great hitters in front of them), but it also tells us nothing about the context of when the run-scoring hits were delivered. If Player A has a four-RBI night in his team's 16–5 loss, and Player B has a two-RBI night in his team's 2–1 victory, who had the better night, in terms of actual impact on the outcome?

Where WPA comes up clutch (pun intended) is its calculation of context. It evolved from a concept called Player Win Averages put forth by Eldon and Harlan Mills and included in *The Hidden Game of Baseball* by John Thorn and Pete Palmer in 1984. They created the stat in an effort to determine if clutch hitting actually existed. And decades of WPA data lends credence to the idea that it does not. A player's WPA one year is unlikely to be predictive of what it will be the next.

So we use WPA to tell us what *has* happened, not what *will* happen. And the former is plenty good enough. Used in conjunction with all the other individual metrics we've covered in this book—on both the hitting and pitching side—it'll help you understand not just what a player contributed in a given season but when. It utilizes the Win Probability data we discussed in Section 4.

As you can see (and could have guessed) from the Carter example, his famous home run had a dramatic impact (+0.66) on his team's Win Probability, coming as it did with the Blue Jays trailing, 6–5, with one out in the bottom of the ninth. On the other end of the spectrum, teammate Roberto Alomar's RBI triple in the ninth inning of the Blue Jays' 10–3 win in Game Three had a WPA of 0.0, because it had no bearing on the result of the ballgame.

WPA is a zero-sum equation. At the end of the game, the winning team's players will have a total WPA of +0.5, and the losing team's players will have a total WPA of -0.5. So every outcome within the game will have a symmetrical impact on the pitcher and hitter. If the pitcher gives up a home run, his WPA will decrease in direct proportion to the amount the hitter's WPA goes up.

A season WPA is a cumulative score of all of the given player's game-by-game WPA marks. With that in mind, here's how FanGraphs describes full-season WPA marks for regular players[6]:

Rating	WPA
Excellent	+6.0
Great	+3.0
Above Average	+2.0
Average	+1.0
Below Average	0.0
Poor	-1.0
Awful	-3.0

You could use WPA as an extra layer of evaluation at awards season. Or—just as fun—as a means of relitigating the past.

The 1961 AL MVP debate between New York Yankees teammates Roger Maris and Mickey Mantle is an all timer. The vote was very close—seven first-place votes and 202 voting points for Maris, and six first-place votes and 198 points for Mantle. The Baltimore Orioles' Jim Gentile (five first-place votes, 157 points) and the Detroit Tigers' Norm Cash (one first-place vote, 151 points) also figured into the voting, but Maris-Mantle is the debate that has endured. These are the stats voters would have been paying the most attention to at the time:

---

6 Keep in mind that players with regular playing time will have more opportunities to accrue WPA than those who are part-timers or who miss time due to injury. And starting pitchers will have more opportunity than relievers.

Player	G	BA	HRs	RBIs
Maris	161	.269	61	141
Mantle	153	.317	54	128

It's not hard to understand why the vote went the way it did. Maris broke Babe Ruth's single-season home-run record, while Mantle missed six of the last nine games of the season due to an abscessed hip. Maris shone through all the scrutiny and, even though his batting average was inferior to that of Mantle, he delivered more homers and drove in more runs, including 21 to Mantle's 14 in the September homestretch, when the Yankees were nailing down the AL pennant. Surely, he was more clutch, correct?

If only they knew then what we know now. Not only was Mantle far superior to Maris in OPS (1.135 to .993), OPS+ (206 to 167), and wRC+ (196 to 162), but he was also the more clutch one, per WPA:

Player	MLB (in 1961)	All-Time
Mantle	8.97 (1st)	12th
Maris	7.00 (4th)	T-94th

WPA can also cast a different light on a player's season than what the public might perceive. For example, there was much fanfare—or perhaps we should call it phanphare—when Bryce Harper joined the Phillies prior to the 2019 season on a whopping 13-year, $330 million contract. So when the 26-year-old Harper had a good-but-not-MVP-caliber first year in Philly, some considered it a disappointment. His wRC+ ranked a ho-hum 44th among major-league qualifiers.

But WPA painted Harper in a different light. There, he tied for sixth in all of baseball with a 4.6 mark, per Baseball Reference.

Was that clutchness, or randomness? You can make your own judgment. But at least Harper made his hits count.

So Much Clutch

The all-time WPA leader is Barry Bonds, and by a healthy margin. According to Baseball Reference, Bonds was worth 127.66 total WPA, 26.57 points higher than his next-closest competition—his godfather, Willie Mays.

Bonds also has the three highest single-season WPA marks on record: in 2002 (10.50), 2001 (11.48), and the all-time high in 2004 (12.96). The only other players with at least 10 WPA in a season are the San Francisco Giants' Willie McCovey in 1969 (10.12) and the Philadelphia A's Al Simmons in 1930 (10.33).

WAR (WINS ABOVE REPLACEMENT)

What it is: *A measure of a player's value in all facets of the game by determining how many more "wins" he is worth than a readily available replacement at the same position.*

What it is not: *Armed conflict.*

How it is calculated: *The formula is different for position players and pitchers . . .*

For position players: (The number of runs above average a player is worth in his batting, baserunning, and fielding + adjustment for position + adjustment for league + the number of runs provided by a replacement-level player) / Runs per Win[7]

For pitchers: Different WAR equations use either Runs Allowed per Nine Innings Pitched or Fielding Independent Pitching (FIP). Those numbers are adjusted for league and ballpark. Then, using league averages, it is determined how many wins a pitcher was worth based on those numbers and his innings pitched total.

Though other versions exist (and teams also have their own proprietary models), by far the two predominant versions of WAR in the public sphere are Baseball Reference's bWAR (sometimes

---

7 Runs per Win is based on the run environment in a given season. Think of it this way: If an 81–81 team has a Run Differential of zero, what would you expect the Run Differential to be for a team that is 82–80? The answer varies by year, but generally falls between 9 and 11 runs per win.

labeled rWAR) and FanGraphs' fWAR. While the framework for each method is generally the same, the hitting, pitching, and fielding metrics used to calculate them differ. For instance, with regard to fielding, Baseball Reference uses Defensive Runs Saved (DRS), while FanGraphs uses Ultimate Zone Rating (UZR). This is why a player can have two different WAR totals listed on two different sites.

For our example, we'll use FanGraphs' position player calculation, which relies on the sort of run estimators referenced in the Runs Created (RC) chapter. While, as with most of the stats in this book, there is little chance anybody reading this will ever try to calculate a player's WAR on their own, at least this will shed a little light on what goes into the equation:

Example: *Stan Musial, 1948 St. Louis Cardinals*

Batting Runs	*Baserunning Runs*	*Fielding Runs*
86.4	*1.1*	*5.0*

Positional Adjustment	*League Adjustment*	*Replacement Runs*
4.7	*1.7*	*20.9*

Runs per Win
9.963

62.2 + 8.2 + 1.6 - 1.2 + 2.8 + 20.5 / 9.264

110.4 / 9.963

Musial's 1948 fWAR was 11.1.

Why it matters: *Because it is the most readily available, all-encompassing evaluation tool, ranking players across positions and quantifying each player's value in terms of a specific number of wins.*

Where you can find it: *Baseball Reference and FanGraphs.*

Some years back, the need to settle disputes, the desire to exert influence, and the insuppressible advancement of ideological change led the baseball world to WAR. In the time since, though not recognized as an official stat by Major League Baseball or the Elias Sports Bureau, WAR has managed to weave its way into casual conversation and everyday analysis.

But it has also managed to inspire a lot of ridicule, a lot of confusion, and, worst of all, a lot of lame Edwin Starr[8] references from unoriginal sportswriters ("WAR, what is it good for? Absolutely nothin'!").

WAR emanated from discussions in the sabermetric community during the 1980s. While around in some form or fashion for more than thirty years, it really gained public prominence during the American League MVP debate involving Miguel Cabrera and Mike Trout back in 2012 (more on that below). But there remains a wide swath of baseball fans who look at it as nothing more than alphabet soup. This explainer is for them.

The basic concept of WAR is as follows: If you formed a team of freely available minor leaguers (a.k.a. "replacement-level talent"), it wouldn't win many games. In fact, estimates used for WAR peg that number of wins at 48, which is roughly a .300 winning percentage over the course of a 162-game season. Though that's better than the infamous 1899 Cleveland Spiders (20–134 record, .130 winning percentage), it shouldn't be something teams strive for.

So if you took Player A from that replacement-level club and replaced him with Free Agent X, and the club won 54 games instead of 48, that means that Free Agent X was worth 6 WAR, because the team improved by six games with him on the roster.

WAR, therefore, estimates a player's total value to his team and uses a concept everybody can understand—wins—to relay that value. Here, based on data from the last decade, are the basic rules

---

8 That Starr has "win" within his first name is either the universe speaking to us or, you know, just a coincidence.

of WAR for position players and starting pitchers (relievers generally don't accrue enough innings to post significant WAR marks):

Quality of Player	WAR
MVP Material	8 or higher
Superstar	6–8
All-Star	4–6
Solid Regular	2–4
Role Player	1–2
Bench Material	0–1
Triple-A Material	0 or below

WAR distills various contributing factors into a single number.
It really isn't so much a stat itself as more of a Frankenstein-like
accumulation of other stats molded into one. Thanks to its acces-
sibility, it has served as a sort of gateway drug for curious folks
just setting foot into sabermetrics. Thanks to its application across
eras, it has heightened the Hall of Fame discussion (more on that
below, too). And thanks to the embrace it has received over time
from the writers and TV broadcasters covering baseball, it has
become, for better or worse, an almost de facto decider in the
comparison of position players for the annual MVP votes.

WAR's biggest impact, however, is the influence it wields in
modern front offices. While WAR is far from the only factor guiding the decision-making process, in the twenty-first century it did
become a big one, with teams using their own proprietary calculation of player value. They might not call it WAR, and it might be a
more precise measurement than the publicly available WAR data,
but, ultimately, the concept is the same.

"The main value, particularly on the position-player side, is to
be able to capture all the contributions of the player and really do
an apples-to-apples comparison," San Francisco Giants president
of baseball operations Farhan Zaidi told MLB.com in 2019. "So

you're not saying, 'This guy is a plus hitter, but he's below average on the bases and in the field.' We can just say he's a 2 Wins Above Replacement player, taking all that into account."

You can protest WAR, and many have. Complex thinkers have derided it as too simple, and simple thinkers have derided it as too complex. At this point, though, every team in baseball is employing some sort of WAR calculation. In fact, the WAR concept was a major contributing factor in the freeze-out many players north of thirty have experienced in recent free-agent markets. With teams able to put a more finite number on what players have contributed recently—and what, based on that prior performance and established aging curves across the sport, they can reasonably be expected to contribute moving forward—it became more commonplace for teams to go with younger, cheaper, and in some cases higher-upside options within their system. In other words, veterans who were only forecast to be worth in the vicinity of 1 WAR or less were mostly deemed expendable.

That's what WAR has meant for front offices. But what should it mean for us?

Well, to be very clear: WAR has flaws. And we'll get into them in just a little bit. But if nothing else, it's a quick and dirty starting point when discussing players and trying to get a sense of their total contribution to a club.

A player might have a 150 wRC+ but might also be a total train wreck defensively and on the basepaths. WAR will reflect both the good and bad with that particular player. He will gain points for the bat and lose points for the other stuff. Conversely, WAR will also conceivably demonstrate how much a light-hitting shortstop with a great glove makes up for the outs he creates at the plate with the outs he converts in the field. You can use WAR to make a fair comparison of the defensive-minded shortstop with the burly slugging DH to determine which player would have brought more value to a random ballclub.

WAR is also applied to pitchers, meaning you can technically use it to compare the relative values of, say, an ace arm and a big bat. Actually, that's how WAR essentially started, with Bill James attempting to compare the 1986 seasons of Roger Clemens and Don Mattingly in his 1987 *Baseball Abstract*. The concept took shape with the help of various sabermetric minds in the years that followed.

The two main WAR calculations—Baseball Reference and FanGraphs—vary more widely with pitchers than position players, so you'll find larger discrepancies there. In 2018, for example, Philadelphia Phillies pitcher Aaron Nola had a 5.4 fWAR (FG), which ranked fourth in the NL. But his bWAR (BR) was 10.5, higher even than that of Cy Young–winner Jacob deGrom (9.6) of the New York Mets. The reason was that Baseball Reference's baseline was runs allowed (Nola allowed 2.42 runs per nine innings), whereas FanGraphs' baseline was FIP (and Nola had a 3.01 mark). So Baseball Reference was going off what Nola actually allowed, while FanGraphs was going off what he conceivably *should have* allowed based on his strikeout, walk, and homer profile. You can decide which method you prefer and search each site accordingly.

WAR is based on the concept of linear weights. Perhaps without realizing it, you've already learned about linear weights over the course of reading this book. Stats such as wOBA and FIP assign weights to different outcomes (i.e., doubles are more valuable than singles and homers more valuable than doubles). The ingredients in the recipe for position player WAR—things like Batting Runs and Baserunning Runs, Fielding Runs, etc.—operate on those same principles. They assign an average run value to each event in which a player is involved, based on historical averages. Adjustments are made based on the player's position and the value of easily available (read: free) replacements (these values adjust from year to year, based on the league environment). Runs are transformed into wins, with 10 runs representing a single win.

The aforementioned 2012 MVP debate was how many casual consumers were first introduced to WAR, and Trout became the poster boy for a concept he had never previously given any thought to (what with him being singularly focused on becoming one of the greatest players of all time).

Trout had taken his lumps in 40 games at the big-league level down the stretch in 2011 and began 2012 in Triple-A. But once he was promoted on April 28, he proved far more polished, and the results were nothing short of extraordinary. Trout did it all: hitting for power and for average, stealing bases and taking the extra base, reaching over walls to snag would-be home runs, you name it. He was the total package. And while you could pick out a multitude of individual numbers that illustrated why he was special—the .963 OPS, the 49 stolen bases, the 65 extra-base hits, the 19 Defensive Runs Saved (DRS)—it was WAR, the total accumulation, that did the best job of putting his contributions in context. Because to fully appreciate Trout, you had to fully appreciate that he had instantly asserted himself as arguably one of the best players in the game in every major facet (batting, fielding, and running). Only WAR could properly summarize a player like that.

Whether you viewed the Baseball Reference or FanGraphs WAR calculation that year, the fact of the matter was that Trout had eclipsed 10 WAR—an accomplishment often only reserved for Hall of Fame types at the peak of their careers—and he did it despite not even being in the big leagues the first three weeks of the season (thereby giving him fewer games to compile a big WAR number).

There was just one little problem: While Trout was all-everything (the only player, in fact, to finish in the top 10 across the majors in Batting Runs, Fielding Runs, and Baserunning Runs), Cabrera led the AL in the three categories that were still reflexively worshiped by fans and MVP voters alike.

That's right, our old friends batting average, home runs, and RBIs. Baseball's Holy Trinity.

As we discussed back in the first section of this book, the Triple Crown, for all its allure, is actually kind of silly when you think about it. Not just because of the flaws of batting average and RBIs but because a high home run total directly influences a high-RBI total, which is why it is not at all unusual for a league's home run leader to also be its RBI leader. The categories simply are not distinct enough to tell us anything meaningful, and yet they make up 66.666 percent of the Triple Crown.

So, anyway, Cabrera, with a .330 average, 44 homers, and 139 RBIs (not to mention a major league–best .999 OPS), won the Triple Crown. And that was fun and interesting and unusual, occurring as it did for the first time in forty-five years. But by no means should it have been a direct one-way ticket to the MVP. Cabrera was a monster at the plate, yes. But the entirety of his value rested in what he did with his bat. He was not an agile base-runner (-7.5 BsR) or gifted with the glove (-4 DRS at third base). He was a lumbering slugger. And his offensive achievements, while extraordinary, did not exactly run laps around those of Trout. Actually, take all offensive contributions into account and make the necessary ballpark and league adjustments and Trout bested Cabrera in wRC+, 167 to 166. But even if wRC+ didn't matter to a fan or voter infatuated with Cabrera's gaudy Holy Trinity totals, were they really superior enough to totally ignore all of Trout's contributions on the bases and in the field? That would be lunacy. Baseball isn't the Home Run Derby. It's a game that relies on run-suppression as much as run-production, and it's a game in which runs can be produced a wide variety of ways. Trout brought way more value to his ballclub, and WAR illustrated that:

Trout: 10.5 bWAR, 10.1 fWAR,
Cabrera: 7.1 bWAR, 7.3 fWAR

Not even close.[9]

Well, you know how this turned out: Cabrera won in a landslide, with 22 first-place votes to Trout's six. But my best guess, based on how voter attitudes toward WAR have changed in the time since (the fact that Trout's rookie year has proven to be far from a fluke has hopefully legitimized what it was telling us in 2012 in the minds of many), that the vote would be much closer today. Or who knows? Maybe Trout would be the one to win in a landslide. And rightly so.

It would be interesting to know what the Hall of Fame would look like, were WAR available from the beginning of the voting process.

Center fielder Lloyd Waner, for example, has the lowest career bWAR (24.1) of any Hall of Fame position player whose career began in 1900 or later. The younger brother of Paul Waner (a legitimate Hall of Famer with a 72.8 career bWAR) was voted in by the Veterans Committee, largely on the might of the .316 career BA he posted from 1927 to 1945. But his career OPS+ of 99 is essentially league average.

Meanwhile, second baseman Lou Whitaker, who played from 1977 to 1995, has a career bWAR of 75.1—the highest of any Hall-eligible position player from the modern era who has not been tied to performance-enhancing drugs. Whitaker's career WAR is higher than that of Reggie Jackson, Derek Jeter, and his former infield mate Alan Trammell, who was elected into the Hall in 2018. I suspect "Sweet Lou," like Trammell, will get in via the small

---

9   And while some people pointed to team performance—Cabrera's Detroit Tigers won the AL Central, while Trout's Los Angeles Angels finished out of the running for the wild card—the Angels actually had one more win than the Tigers while playing in a much more difficult division. The Angels' Simple Rating System (SRS) score was 0.7, while the Tigers' was 0.4.

committee vote eventually, but WAR insists that selection should have come much earlier. His only year of eligibility on the BBWAA ballot was in 2001, when he appeared on just 2.9 percent of submitted ballots and fell off (5 percent is required to remain on the ballot for the following year). He also, unfortunately, fell short of selection in his first appearance on the Modern Baseball Era Ballot in 2019.

Looking at pitchers, the low WAR watermark for an inducted Hall of Famer is Bob Lemon's 37.6 bWAR from 1946 to 1958. He was ushered in by the BBWAA in 1976, his 14th year on the ballot (players have since been limited to 10 tries on the ballot). Compare that to the 68.1 bWAR Rick Reuschel compiled from 1972 to 1991. Reuschel pitched to a 114 ERA+ across 3,548 1/3 innings, but he was generally on terrible teams with terrible defenses, so his contributions might not have been fully appreciated. He was on the BBWAA ballot just once, in 1997, and appeared on only two of 473 submitted ballots.[10]

While WAR has given us an even greater appreciation for Trout's breathtaking career and deepened the Hall debate, nobody should espouse it as a kink-free concoction. The fog of WAR is real. Offense and baserunning remain easier to calculate than defense, and WAR has often been accused of giving too much weight to faulty defensive data. Furthermore, in the WAR calculation, a home run–robbing catch in the ninth inning of a close game counts the same as a catch well in front of the wall in the middle of a blowout.

To that point, even James has criticized WAR for being context neutral. Win Probability Added (WPA) attempts to demonstrate

---

10 For a deeper dive into the Hall of Fame debate, I strongly recommend the work of Jay Jaffe, a sabermetrician currently working for FanGraphs who developed the JAWS (Jaffe War Score System) to measure a player's Hall worthiness based on both career WAR and seven-year peak WAR (i.e., the seven best seasons of a player's career). Sortable JAWS charts are available at Baseball Reference.

how players performed in the so-called "clutch," and James and others wish WAR would operate more similarly—to, for all intents and purposes, work backward from wins rather than forward from runs.

And let's be honest. It would sure be nice if everybody could agree on a single way of calculating WAR so that we don't have to cite multiple numbers for a single player in a single season.[11]

So maybe WAR is not always the answer. But, like it or not, it has become intrinsic in the language of the game. And it seeks to do what no stat we grew up with ever accomplished: examine a player's total body of work to determine how much he helps a team win a game, and deliver that data cleanly and conveniently. That's a noble cause. And if I had to make a judgment on a player based entirely on his Wins Above Replacement mark or his batting average, well, sign me up for WAR.

All-Time bWAR Leaders (since 1901)

1. 182.4: Babe Ruth
2. 164.3: Walter Johnson
3. 163.6: Cy Young
4. 162.8: Barry Bonds
5. 156.4: Willie Mays
6. 151.0: Ty Cobb
7. 143.0: Hank Aaron
8. 139.2: Roger Clemens
9. 134.0: Tris Speaker
10. 130.8: Honus Wagner
11. 128.2: Stan Musial
12. 127.0: Rogers Hornsby
13. 124.0: Eddie Collins
14. 123.1: Ted Williams
15. 118.9: Grover Cleveland Alexander
16. 117.8: Alex Rodriguez
17. 116.1: Kid Nichols
18. 112.4: Lou Gehrig
19. 111.2: Rickey Henderson
20. 110.3: Mickey Mantle
21. 109.9: Tom Seaver
22. 107.8: Mel Ott
23. 107.4: Nap Lajoie
24. 107.3: Frank Robinson
25. 107.0: Lefty Grove

---

11 Alas, widespread agreement on anything—baseball or otherwise—is difficult to come by.

Position Player Single-Season bWAR Leaders (since 1901)

1. 14.1: Babe Ruth, 1923 New York Yankees
2. 12.9: Babe Ruth, 1921 New York Yankees
3. 12.5: Carl Yastrzemski, 1967 Boston Red Sox
4. 12.4: Babe Ruth, 1927 New York Yankees
5. 12.1: Rogers Hornsby, 1924 St. Louis Cardinals
6. 11.9: Babe Ruth, 1920 New York Yankees
7. 11.9: Barry Bonds, 2001 San Francisco Giants
8. 11.8: Lou Gehrig, 1927 New York Yankees
9. 11.8: Barry Bonds, 2002 San Francisco Giants
10. 11.7: Babe Ruth, 1924 New York Yankees

A-Mays-ing

One player who certainly would have benefited from the availability of a WAR-like metric during his playing days was Willie Mays . . . not that Mays wasn't appreciated in his time nor that he had any trouble waltzing into the Hall of Fame.

But WAR helps illustrate that the "Say Hey Kid" was certifiably robbed of a would-be MVP honor multiple times. Over a 13-season span, from 1954 to 1966, Mays averaged 9.5 bWAR per season yet won the MVP only twice (in '54 and '65). He led his league (all of baseball, in fact) in bWAR in both of those MVP years, but he also led his league in bWAR in '55, '57, '58, '60, '62, '63, and '64. Mays's godson holds the all-time record with seven MVP Awards (Barry Bonds, if you were unaware), but there is a very strong argument that Mays himself should have won at least nine times.

Epilogue
Stats All, Folks?

Baseball Analytics Have Come a Long Way, Baby. But How Much Further Can They Go?

In the *Book of Ecclesiastes*, it is written that, "What has been will be again, what has been done will be done again; there is nothing new under the sun."

In an 1899 edition of the British humor magazine *Punch*, it is the claim of a boy responding to a man hoping to have a patent examined that "everything that can be invented has been invented."

In a 1998 Barenaked Ladies song, it is asserted by the Canadian pop quartet that "It's All Been Done."

I won't go so far as to make such a claim about baseball stats. They're going to keep coming. They're going to keep getting more nuanced. They're going to keep enlightening some folks and befuddling others.

That said, I do wonder if the biggest revelations and revolutions in the world of baseball metrics are mostly behind us. The Bill James reassessments that spawned all sorts of statistics featured in this book has had the effect of absolutely altering opinions on players who might have been cast to the fringes or the farm systems in generations past. These days, you can be a .230 hitter, but your value can be finely articulated—and widely understood—in other ways. That's a seismic sea change from what we grew up with.

And when Statcast came along in 2015, it was the biggest of big data developments, exposing both the average fan and the front offices to more precise ball-tracking and player-movement measurements—and even a new, commonly communicated language (Exit Velocity, Launch Angle, etc.). Though it is undoubtedly a work in progress, it has fundamentally refashioned the way the game is written about and broadcast. And, most importantly, it has changed the way the players themselves assess their skill sets and seek to improve.

So where do we go from here?

Well, the changes of the future are likely to be more incremental than monumental. But for starters, we've got a long way to go before anybody can confidently claim that the publicly available defensive measurements are definitive (catching defense has proven particularly difficult to quantify). The hardware used for Statcast measurements changed in 2020—from Trackman to Hawk-Eye, which is also used to track serves in tennis—and that has the benefit of more accurately tracking player limbs, arm angles, arm actions, etc. Statcast also unveiled an infield defense measurement prior to the 2020 season, helping us further understand the effects of positioning and shifts.

All of the above is going to sharpen the defensive stats, which will conceivably, in turn, sharpen Wins Above Replacement. The more reliable the defensive portion of the equation becomes, the better WAR can be at relaying player value, as Mike Petriello, MLB.com's resident Statcast analyst explains.

> The framework of WAR is pretty good. Its biggest weakness is that there is more than one version. But I think people have caught onto it reasonably well. Everybody understands a player's value is not just his average or his OPS or whatever. His value can be determined in a lot of ways, and WAR tries to get that to one number.

The biggest change will be with the inputs. Whether it's Statcast or something else, as we figure out a better way to evaluate defense than UZR, it will improve the outcome product.[1]

Statcast is also helping player ratings become more relatable for a generation of fans who grew up playing games like *MLB: The Show*, where player skill sets are broken down into categories such as "Arm," "Field," "React," "Steal," and "Power," and then added up into a single score. Because the on-field measurements are increasingly acute, the data behind these assessments is more meaningful. There are so many directions it can take us in the coming years as the "lab technicians," as we'll refer to them here, aim it at mostly untapped elements such as catcher defense and baserunning. The accuracy and availability of its data will continue to increase. If you are the intellectually curious sort who would like to know what's going on in the Statcast lab, you can check out the MLB Technology blog at technology.mlblogs.com. There, data scientists, software engineers, and other industry experts share their insights into how analytics are impacting the sport both on and off the field, in everything from scheduling to ticket sales.

But at the risk of echoing *Ecclesiastes* (or being asked to join the Barenaked Ladies), the cornerstones of advanced baseball metrics are already in place. Thanks to curious and creative observers with brilliant brains, we've crossed some sort of great divide. We have better understanding of what *should have* happened vs. what *actually* happened. We can more keenly convey

---

1 I can't recommend Petriello's work enough (in both print and broadcast). He will routinely give you expert insight into what we're watching and make you think about the game in a different way. And he didn't even pay me to put this here.

underlying skill sets that can be skewed by bad luck and, therefore, aren't necessarily communicated by the outcome stats.

So it's folly to genuflect at the altar of the Holy Trinity of batting average, homers, and RBIs while plugging your ears and closing your eyes to anything else. Attend a major-league game today, and you're likely to see, at the very least, a player's OPS broadcast in big, bold letters on the scoreboard. If you think about it, that, in itself, is a significant step forward from where we were even a decade ago. The infiltration of the modern metrics into the ballpark and broadcast experience is only going to grow in the coming years, and hopefully this book has prepared you for that.

As I stated from the beginning, I understand—and myself even sometimes succumb to—the charm and attraction of the stats that have been around forever. I get why fans like numbers that end in fives and tens, why they more easily relate to benchmarks like 20 wins or .300 averages or 100 RBIs totals. The sport's connective tissue across generations is an inherent, immense part of its appeal.

But hopefully, in this book, I've helped demonstrate how the modern math strengthens, not severs, that connective tissue. It can help us relitigate past arguments, confirm what we already expected, or uncover something we might have missed. And when analyzing the game of the present day, it can give us a greater appreciation for and comprehension of what we're watching, placing everything in the proper context. Accessing and discerning the data that teams are using to build their rosters and that players are using to assess their seasons ought to help us get a higher percentage of enjoyment out of the baseball-viewing experience.

Then again, I'm not sure I could put a number to it . . .

Quiz
The Numbers Game

Time to put your money where your math is. Test your comprehension of some of the lessons learned in this book by attempting to knock this quiz out of the park.

Where's Dan "Quiz"enberry when you need him?

QUESTIONS

1. Which of these batters had the higher on-base percentage in 1938?
   Charlie Gehringer, Detroit Tigers: .306/.425/.486 slash line
   Joe Medwick, St. Louis Cardinals: .322/.369/.536 slash line

2. Which of these pitchers was helped more by his defense in 1976?
   Dennis Eckersley, Cleveland Indians: 3.43 ERA, 101 ERA+, 2.72 FIP, 1.17 WHIP
   Mark Fidrych, Detroit Tigers: 2.34 ERA, 159 ERA+, 3.15 FIP, 1.08 WHIP

3. Which team rated better defensively in 2018?
   Tampa Bay Rays: 0.3 SRS, .722 DER, 2.73 PADE, +70 Diff
   Atlanta Braves: 0.6 SRS, .722 DER, 1.71 PADE, +102 Diff

4. Hack Wilson had a career .307/.395/.545 slash line with a 144 OPS+ and 143 wRC+. What was his career OPS?

5. Which player had the higher career Isolated Power (ISO) mark?
   Manny Ramirez: .312/.411/.585 slash
   Jim Thome: .276/.402/.554 slash

6. Which of these hitters had more batted-ball luck in 2019?
   Ian Kinsler, San Diego Padres: .217 BA, .646 OPS, .280 wOBA, .247 xwOBA, 70 OPS+
   Yadier Molina, St. Louis Cardinals: .270 BA, 711 OPS, .306 wOBA, .320 xwOBA, 85 OPS+

7. Which pitcher fared better than the league average in the 1988 season?
   Bret Saberhagen, Kansas City Royals: 3.80 ERA, 3.51 FIP, 96 ERA-, 1.27 WHIP, 68.7 LOB%
   Nolan Ryan, Houston Astros: 3.52 ERA, 3.04 FIP, 105 ERA-, 1.24 WHIP, 71.4 LOB%

8. Which third baseman provided more offensive value during his career?
   Scott Rolen (1996–2012): .281/.364/.490 slash, 70.2 bWAR, 21.2 dWAR
   Ron Santo (1960–74): .277/.362/.464 slash, 70.5 bWAR, 8.7 dWAR

9. When Warren Spahn of the Milwaukee Braves won the Cy Young Award in 1957, he had a 4.8 bWAR but a 2.7 fWAR.

   True or False: Spahn's 1957 ERA was lower than his FIP.

10. Which outfielder more greatly impacted the 2005 Reds' likelihood of winning games over the course of the season?

    Adam Dunn: 138 wRC+, 4.27 WPA, 4.1 BsR, 3.3 fWAR, 140 OPS+

    Ken Griffey Jr.: 142 wRC+, 3.22 WPA, -0.6 BsR, 2.9 fWAR, 144 OPS+

Bonus! Which player had more Dingers Created in 1962?

Hank Aaron: .618 SLG, .296 ISO, 45 HRs, .304 BABIP, 1.008 OPS

Willie Mays: .615 SLG, .311 ISO, 49 HRs, .286 BABIP, .999 OPS

ANSWERS

1. Charlie Gehringer. His .425 OBP is represented in the second section of his slash line, with the first being batting average and the third being slugging percentage.

2. Mark Fidrych. The 0.81-point differential between his 3.15 FIP and 2.34 ERA means his supporting cast helped him suppress more runs than his strikeouts, unintentional walks, hit by pitches, and homers allowed would lead you to expect. Eckersley, on the other hand, had his ERA inflated (from 2.72 to 3.43) by factors (like defense) that were out of his control.

3. The Rays. While the Braves rated more strongly in Simple Rating System (SRS) and Run Differential (Diff) and had an identical Defensive Efficiency Rating (DER), the Rays had the superior Park Adjusted Defensive Efficiency (PADE).

4. Hack Wilson's career OPS was .940—the sum of his OBP (.395) and SLG (.545).

5. Jim Thome. His SLG (.554) minus his BA (.276) is .278, while Ramirez's (.585 - .312) is .273.

6. Ian Kinsler. Even though Yadier Molina's offensive season was stronger across the board, Molina's xwOBA (.320), based on quality of contact, insists that his .306 wOBA should have been slightly higher. Kinsler, meanwhile, had an actual wOBA that exceeded his xwOBA.

7. Bret Saberhagen. Even though Nolan Ryan had the lower ERA, FIP, and WHIP, and the higher LOB%, Saberhagen's ERA- (96) was four percentage points below the league average, while Ryan's was five points higher than the league average. Remember that the goal with ERA- is to be below 100, while the goal with ERA+ is to be above it (Saberhagen's ERA+ was 106, while Ryan's was 94). The key difference here was the league environment. In Saberhagen's AL, there were 4.36 runs per game, as opposed to the 3.88 per game scored in Ryan's NL.

8. Ron Santo. Though each segment of his slash line was slightly below that of Scott Rolen and his bWAR was virtually identical, Santo had a lower percentage of his WAR tally attributed to his glove. He had a 8.7 Defensive WAR (dWAR) compared to Rolen's 21.2 mark, and his offensive contributions also carry

more weight because he played in an era with less run scoring than Rolen did.

9. True. The fWAR calculation uses FIP (or essentially what his ERA should have been), whereas the bWAR calculation uses actual earned runs allowed. So the giveaway here was that Spahn's fWAR was so much lower than his bWAR. Sure enough, Spahn's 2.69 ERA was nearly a full point lower than his 3.63 FIP, which is why he rated so much better on the bWAR scale.

10. Adam Dunn. His 4.27 Win Probability Added (WPA) was more than a full point higher than Griffey's. (But as the beat writer covering this team for MLB.com, I can tell you those Reds didn't win much.)

Bonus! Willie Mays, duh. He hit more homers!

HOW MANY DID YOU GET RIGHT?

0: Welp, at least you are capable of calculating your batting average. (It's .000.)

1 or 2: Take a walk, a nap, get some coffee, and then read the book again.

3 or 4: You have some flaws, though not as many as the win and save rules.

5 or 6: You're making progress, like a team sweeping a late-August series and lowering its Magic Number.

7 or 8: You are ready to apply for the Branch Rickey Memorial Internship Program (if it existed).

9 or 10: Bill James should have you on speed dial.

11: You are officially and unmistakably a nerd. Congrats!

Acknowledgments

Throughout my time writing about baseball, I have heard from many readers (like the former CPA and financial analyst referenced in the introduction), friends, and family members who are frustrated by the increasing prevalence of advanced stats in coverage of the game. And so I owe them a big debt of gratitude for ultimately guiding the conversation that takes place in these pages. My hope was to make what is complicated more relatable and to demonstrate that, when applied properly, these stats can heighten—not hinder—our love of the game.

It was my editor, Jason Katzman, who had the idea of putting all these statistical pieces together in one place and making this book digestible and easy to reference when a need for explanation arises. Big thanks to him for spearheading this effort, encouraging me to give it a go, and assisting with his research and helpful edits along the way. Thanks also to the rest of the team at Sports Publishing for pushing this project across the plate.

Thanks to Tony Petitti, Gregg Klayman, Matt Meyers, and Jim Banks of Major League Baseball and MLB.com for giving me the approval and flexibility I needed to write this book while fulfilling my full-time duties at the best baseball site on the planet. And thanks to all my MLB.com colleagues, past and present, for deepening my appreciation for what we do with the comradeship we've created.

Special thanks to Mike Petriello for his help with this project and to the rest of MLB.com's Statcast "lab techs" and researchers for all they do to make myself and others smarter than we used to be.

This book would not be possible if not for the overwhelming trove of data available at sites like FanGraphs and Baseball Reference. At times, this book felt like an (unpaid) advertisement for those two sites, in particular, and I hope I've done my small part to direct any baseball fans who may not have been fully aware of their offerings to them. Added thanks to FanGraphs managing editor Meg Rowley for her graciousness in allowing us to reprint FanGraphs' rules of thumbs for various stats in this book so that readers could readily reference them.

So many incredible sportswriters unknowingly contributed to this project just by doing what they do best. The greats like Joe Posnanski, Jayson Stark, Ken Rosenthal, and Tom Verducci are especially gifted at weaving the numbers into the narrative, and closely following the work of these wordsmiths over the course of my own career has aided my understanding of many of the stats contained herein while continually pushing me to improve my own coverage and to always dig deeper. Thanks to them for the inspiration.

Many thanks to my friend and mentor, Justice B. Hill, who always saw the best in me and my work and was directly responsible for my first opportunities in baseball journalism.

Keith Law's *Smart Baseball* was an important reference point when shaping this project. Ultimately, I wanted this book to differ from Law's by operating more as a glossary; a handy reference guide that can be consumed quickly. But Law's deeper dive into how and why baseball has come to embrace "Big Data" and where this is all headed is—appropriately, given the title—smartly written and highly recommended.

Thanks to the many front office executives, managers, players, and other baseball personnel—far too many to list here—who have both helped me understand the numbers and never let me forget that the game is about more than numbers. For them, I tried to write this book with both head and heart.

Thanks to my family and friends for their encouragement. Thanks to Bruce Springsteen, just because. And above all else, all my love and thanks to my wife, Kate, and daughters, Ella and Lily, for their patience as I put this project together in the midst of a thousand other things. Now we can read this book at bedtime!

Appendix of Analytic Rating Tables
BATTING ANALYTIC RATING TABLES

OBP (On-Base Percentage)

Rating	OBP
Excellent	.390 or above
Great	.370
Above Average	.340
Average	.320
Below Average	.310
Poor	.300
Awful	.290 or below

OPS (On-Base Plus Slugging)

Rating	OPS
Excellent	1.000
Great	.900
Above Average	.800
Average	.700
Below average	.670
Poor	.600
Awful	.570

SLG (Slugging Percentage)

Rating	SLG
Excellent	.550 or above
Great	.500
Above Average	.450
Average	.420
Below Average	.400
Poor	.390
Awful	.380 or below

ISO (Isolated Power)

Rating	ISO
Excellent	.250
Great	.200
Above Average	.170
Average	.140
Below Average	.120
Poor	.100
Awful	.080

wOBA
(Weighted On-Base Average)

Rating	wOBA
Excellent	.390 or above
Great	.370
Above Average	.340
Average	.320
Below Average	.310
Poor	.300
Awful	.290 or below

BsR (Baserunning)

Rating	BsR
Excellent	8
Great	6
Above Average	2
Average	0
Below Average	-2
Poor	-4
Awful	-6

wRC+ (Weighted Runs Created Plus)
OPS+ (On-Base Plus Slugging Plus)

Rating	wRC+ or OPS+
Excellent	160
Great	140
Above Average	115
Average	100
Below Average	80
Poor	75
Awful	60

xSLG (Expected Slugging Percentage)
xwOBA (Expected Weighted On-Base Average)

Rating	xSLG	xwOBA
Excellent	.550 or above	.390 or above
Great	.500	.370
Above Average	.450	.340
Average	.420	.320
Below Average	.400	.310
Poor	.390	.300
Awful	.380 or below	.290 or below

PITCHING ANALYTIC RATING TABLES

ERA+ (Adjusted Earned Run Average)

Rating	ERA+
Excellent	160
Great	130
Above Average	120
Average	100
Below Average	90
Poor	80
Awful	70

WHIP (Walks plus Hits per Inning Pitched)

Rating	WHIP
Excellent	1.00 and under
Great	1.10
Above Average	1.20
Average	1.30
Below Average	1.40
Poor	1.50
Awful	1.60 and higher

GSc (Game Score)

Rating	Game Score
Make Sure Your Friends Are Watching	90–100
Excellent	80–90
Great	70–80
Good	60–70
Above Average	50–60
Below Average	40–50
Poor	30–40
Bad	20–30
Awful	10–20
Unspeakable	0–10

FIP
(Fielding Independent Pitching)

Rating	FIP
Excellent	3.20
Great	3.50
Above Average	3.80
Average	4.20
Below Average	4.40
Poor	4.70
Awful	5.00

K% (Strikeout Rate)
BB% (Walk Rate)

Rating	K%	BB%
Excellent	27.0	4.5
Great	24.0	5.5
Above Average	22.0	6.5
Average	20.0	7.7
Below Average	17.0	8.0
Poor	15.0	8.5
Awful	13.0	9.0

FB% (Fly-Ball Rate)
LD% (Line-Drive Rate)
GB% (Ground-Ball Rate)
IFFB% (Infield Fly Ball Rate)

Rate	League Average
FB	35%
LD	21%
GB	44%
IFFB	11%

K/BB
(Strikeout to Walk Ratio)

Rating	K/BB
Excellent	4.00
Great	3.20
Above Average	2.80
Average	2.50
Below Average	2.20
Poor	1.90
Awful	1.50

HR/FB
(Home Run to Fly Ball Rate)

Rating	HR/FB
Excellent	5.0
Great	7.0
Above Average	8.5
Average	9.5
Below Average	10.5
Poor	11.5
Awful	13.0

LOB%
(Left On Base Percentage)

Rating	LOB%
Excellent	80
Great	78
Above Average	75
Average	72
Below Average	70
Poor	65
Awful	60

IRS%
(Inherited Runs Scored Percentage)

Rating	IRS%
Excellent	20
Great	25
Above Average	28
Average	30
Below Average	33
Poor	38
Awful	40

DEFENSE ANALYTIC RATING TABLES

DRS (Defensive Runs Saved)
UZR (Ultimate Zone Rating) **DER (Defensive Efficiency Rating)**

Rating	DRS or UZR
Excellent	+15
Great	+10
Above Average	+5
Average	0
Below Average	-5
Poor	-10
Awful	-15

Rating	DER
Excellent	.720 or above
Good	.710
Average	.700
Below Average	.690
Terrible	.680 or below

Inside Edge Fielding

Rating	IEF
Routine	90%–100%
Likely	60%–90%
About Even	40%–60%
Unlikely	10%–40%
Impossible	0%

Outs Above Average

Rating	OAA
Excellent	+10 and Up
Great	1 to 9
Average	0
Poor	-1 to -9
Awful	-10 and Under

MISCELLANEOUS ANALYTIC RATING TABLES

WPA (Win Probability Added)

Rating	WPA
Excellent	+6.0
Great	+3.0
Above Average	+2.0
Average	+1.0
Below Average	0.0
Poor	-1.0
Awful	-3.0

WAR (Wins Above Replacement)

Quality of Player	WAR
MVP Material	8 or higher
Superstar	6–8
All-Star	4–6
Solid Regular	2–4
Role Player	1–2
Bench Material	0–1
Triple-A Material	0 or below